AN INTRODUCTION
TO POPE

AN INTRODUCTION
TO POPE

Pat Rogers

Methuen & Co Ltd
11 New Fetter Lane London EC4P 4EE

First published 1975
by Methuen & Co Ltd
11 New Fetter Lane London EC4P 4EE
© *1975 Pat Rogers*
Printed in Great Britain by
Butler & Tanner Ltd, Frome and London

ISBN (hardbound) 0 416 78440 2
ISBN (paperback) 0 416 78450 X

76-360071

Distributed in the USA by
Harper and Row Publishers Inc · Barnes and Noble Import Division

For
Michael & Florence
Treadwell

CONTENTS

PREFACE

The eighteenth century as a whole remains obstinately out of fashion. Yet Pope, the most representative European poet of his age, survives. He has not acquired the easy glamour which novelists attain when their works are made into television serials. But the currency of a classic can take other forms, and the serious study of literature provides a climate for writers of the past to thrive anew. Pope is widely read in advanced school classes, in colleges and universities. When he is read, he is commonly enjoyed. Sometimes the enjoyment begins a little grudgingly (one feels somehow that one ought to be resisting the impact of his subtly contrived effects); but those who come with an open mind and a genuine response to poetry often stay to admire and to share in the pleasures of Pope.

The word 'introduction' is meant to convey something more than a mere neutral guide, or prolegomena to the study of Pope. I have in mind the act of sociable courtesy by which we introduce our friends to one another. It was characteristic of the Augustans to assimilate their intellectual life into the ordinary round of day-to-day activities. They saw writing books as a species of good fellowship, just as they designed 'companionable' buildings and composed agreeable and approachable music. I have neither Augustan expectations to count on, nor Augustan means to fulfil them. But it has been my aim to make the encounter with Pope so far as possible a convivial occasion, rather than an abstract of some remote learned proceedings. There is now a formidable body of scholarship grown up around Pope. I am naturally indebted to this distinguished heritage, but, like Pope, I have tried to use this tradition rather than parade it for its own sake. There are still few places where a reader can meet with a full account of Pope which incorporates the most up-to-date findings and yet assumes no prior knowledge of the poet or his age. In this book I have attempted to take note of the latest research, without drowning the text beneath the wide Scriblerian sea of unwanted learning.

The major items in modern scholarship are threefold. R. H.

Griffith's bibliography was truly excellent in its time; but it now needs replacing, and bears only seldom on the main issues I have treated. George Sherburn's work as biographer and as editor of Pope's correspondence fortunately preserves all its value, and this book has been written with constant recourse to Sherburn in both capacities. However, my principal debt is that shared with all students of Pope. The superb Twickenham edition of the poems was originally undertaken by a team of collaborators headed by John Butt. It was completed after his death by the appearance of a splendid series of volumes devoted to Pope's Homer, edited by the greatest of living Popians, Maynard Mack. I should like to record here my gratitude to the publishers (Methuen & Co., and the Yale University Press) for their enlightened patronage of this venture, at a time when scholarly publishing has often found itself on the retreat.

The Twickenham edition is now in every respect standard. So much so, that I have organized this book according to its layout. After introductory sections on Pope's historical situation and on his art, six chapters are devoted to the major poems. Chapters 3 and 4 correspond respectively to the first and second Twickenham volumes. Chapter 5 includes coverage of the Homer, which makes up the last four volumes in the Twickenham series (i.e. 7–10). Chapter 6 answers to Twickenham III.i and III.ii, and Chapters 7 and 8 apply to the material of Twickenham IV and V. This division is both chronologically and thematically sound, and if anyone should think that such servile adherence to the Twickenham plan distorts my view of Pope's development, I can only reply that – like most contemporary students of Pope – I have lived too long under the generous Twickenham auspices to venture too far without its aid. To act otherwise is like rolling up one's map and setting out across the trackless wastes to discover the source of the Thames. Sensible readers, I believe, would keep such a journey without maps for genuinely uncharted territory. In the case of Pope, thanks to this noble edition, we can forget the pioneer stage and enter his world on privileged terms. We can, in a word, derive civilized enjoyment from the poetry right away.

For abbreviations used in the text, see p. 159.

CHAPTER ONE

The writer and his audience

Alexander Pope is a literary artist of the first rank, whose poems have stood their share of the tests of time – more than their share, perhaps. Unfashionable (though never unread) through much of the nineteenth century, he has come strongly back into favour over the past forty years. Indeed, there has scarcely been a literary fad since the 1920s which has not somehow bent to accommodate Pope. It may be a mixed blessing, of course, to be borne on the wings of a cult, and admiration for the writer has sometimes meant glossing over the faults of the man. Nevertheless, the perennial delights of *The Rape of the Lock,* the enduring interest of *The Dunciad*, the increasingly exciting vistas we see opened up by the *Imitations of Horace*, these all demonstrate a genuine power of survival. Aptly so, for Pope himself had engaged in a constant battle for self-preservation. The wonder is not that he became such a good writer, but that he became one at all.

Born in 1688, he would have enjoyed a comfortable background but for one crucial fact. His family were Roman Catholics; and in the very year of Pope's birth the last Catholic to sit on the British throne, James II, was expelled to France amid national rejoicing. In fact James's failings – as a man, as a king, as a constitutional politician – had relatively little to do with his precise religious beliefs. But Pope inherited an unpopular faith, widely regarded as next door to treasonable, and the condition of an outcast. Papists enjoyed a severely limited range of civil rights. The boy was even brought up first on the outskirts of London, later in the country, largely because his father (who had made his money in the city as a linen draper) was obliged by law to live at a decent remove from the capital. Ever afterwards Pope was struggling back, metaphorically or literally, to the centre of things.[1]

But there was soon a more grievous handicap still. In his early childhood he contracted a tubercular infection which left him permanently stunted, crippled, a prey to disorders such as migraine and asthma. The famous phrase, 'this long Disease, my Life' (*EA*, 131), is less fanciful than cruelly accurate. He was rendered dependent on others for the simplest tasks – such as dressing – and this physical reliance may have produced in compensation the fierce personal independence which did so much to shape his artistic career.[2] And his undoubted prickliness towards other people can fairly be connected with his pain and a sense of his own oddity. In particular, his overstrained attitude to sex, mingling boyish smut with elaborate gallantry, must derive from feelings of being unattractive, if not grotesque, to the women he desired.

Pope, then, grew up in circumstances which threw him back on himself. His parents were both well into middle age (his father had already been widowed once); his half-sister, who was much older, soon married a local landowner named Rackett. His early tutors were recusant priests of little distinction. So he experienced the classic upbringing of the only child. Gifted, ambitious and deeply private by nature, he buried himself in the countryside and in books. The first of these meant the delightful and historically charged 'green Retreats' of Windsor Forest (*WF*, 1), out of which the poet constructed a symbolism of retirement. The second meant principally classical and English poetry. Literature of the ancient world still pervaded Western education; it set standards, prescribed models, and defined attitudes. But it is equally important to remember that Pope developed a passionate interest in vernacular writing, with Shakespeare, Spenser, Milton and Dryden as his masters. Chaucer he came to love, too, though in ways that would now seem eclectic and unscholarly.

Not all Pope's mentors were to be found among the illustrious dead. All his days he had a capacity for something one might call hero worship, were it not too *interested* an emotion for that. What usually happened was that Pope latched on to some older or more powerful figure, conducted a course of self-instruction on his own terms, and then at some point dropped his former pilot, with or without animosity. The list of these guides, philosophers and friends is a long one, and covers some distinguished and some mediocre men. In his adolescence Pope took up with Sir William Trumbull, a retired diplomat who occupied much the same role as did Sir William Temple with Jonathan Swift a few years earlier. Unlike Swift, Pope showed himself highly precocious; and he had soon outgrown the provincial luminaries of Berkshire. To London he must go, like any aspiring writer; and by this time he was ready for such fading coffee house stars as the dramatist William Wycherley (Dryden, alas, had died just too soon) or the worldly man about literature, Henry Cromwell. A whole panel of selected midwives presided over the appearance of the *Pastorals* (published 1709), the first substantial item in the canon. Pope acknowledged the help not only of Trumbull and Wycherley, but also of William Walsh – an intelligent poetaster – Granville, Garth and Maynwaring. The two great patrons, Halifax and Somers, are little more than dignified sponsors; their names constitute a sign of 'By Appointment'. All these men were genuinely interested in the craft of poetry, but by the time Pope had left his teens he had out-distanced them all. He continued to court the rich and successful, but with less and less pretence of seeking their advice. He enjoyed social intercourse with the great, but he never allowed such intimacy to buy off his pen. Social prestige was one thing, his art another.

   The next years witnessed an almost unbroken triumph, with a series of brilliant poems headed by *The Rape of the Lock* bringing Pope's name to the attention of everyone. He joined the glittering array of talent who made up the Scriblerus Club: Swift, John Gay, Dr Arbuthnot and Thomas Parnell. At the same time he got to know the influential Whig writers headed by Joseph Addison and Richard Steele. He embarked on the translation of Homer's *Iliad*, and when it was completed in 1720 he had achieved a competence for life simply from the profits of this work. By this time too he had put down roots in Twickenham: a settled home, and a kind of topographic trademark, for the rest of his life. Here he observed his filial duties, his mother living to an advanced age, cultivated a garden full of symbolic impedimenta and *objets trouvés,* and went on working. His first collected volume had appeared in 1717; and though work on *The Odyssey* and an edition of Shakespeare (1725) slowed him for a time, he burst out around the age of forty with a new flood of satiric masterpieces. It is these later poems, including the *Moral Essays*, Horatian poems and *The Dunciad* in its vari-

ous guises, which enjoy the highest admiration today. Without
prejudging any critical questions, we can say that they develop
logically from the earlier work, more fanciful and less abrasive
though it is. Famous, feared and loved all at once, Pope came
to be regarded as *the* man of letters of his day. His renown
was still at its peak when the ill health he had fought so long
finally overcame his feeble body. He died in 1744, a week after
his fifty-sixth birthday.

To all appearances this is the purest success story. A sickly,
disadvantaged boy pulls himself by his own efforts to high cultural eminence. He acquires a sound financial standing, though
not vulgar riches. He looks after a fond mother; makes a host
of friends, most of whom he keeps; mixes on terms of
unstrained familiarity with the greatest in the land; pays his
double taxes, as a Catholic; and leads a modest, dignified private life. Above all, he keeps writing, and maintains the quality
of his work with astonishing regularity. Really there is nothing
lacking, excepting good health and a lasting sexual relationship – but this last would have worried his contemporaries
much less than would be the case today. Yet to some people
this is all too successful to be convincing. The progress is too
smooth; there are few signs of artistic alienation, and what looks
like a disconcerting readiness to accept the plaudits of polite
society. But this is only half the truth.

In fact, Pope's assent to the received values of his time is
more apparent than real. Much of his work, particularly in
the 1730s, was devoted to countering the new politics of that
period – not just the administrative machine itself, but the
wider moral assumptions on which it rested. From the *Rape*
onwards, Pope made himself into an unrivalled anatomist of
the idiocies and inhumanities of the polite world. His satire
is vigorous, plain spoken, *risqué* on many occasions. Far from
a timeserver, he established a whole new rhetoric of dissent.
Yet it is true that he did all this without, as it were, infringing
his gentlemanly status, or jeopardizing his admission to the best
circles. To understand this, we must look carefully at the actual
form and idiom of Pope's poetry. As I have said elsewhere,
'He was that most dangerous critic of society, who can ape
its fashionable chat and fall in with its pointless conventions.

He wrote of the social scene from within: but he was a fifth-columnist.'[3]

* * * * *

The term 'society' must be handled with care. It does not refer to the entire six million or so people living in England at that time. London was unique in possessing a large, ill-governed, unhealthy urban sprawl, rife with organized crime. Towns such as Liverpool, growing fast though they were, had still not overtaken Bristol and Norwich in population. (When Pope died in 1744 the great mercantile centre of Philadelphia was amongst the leading cities in the British Empire; and the poet's American readership was very considerable throughout the eighteenth century.)[4] Nevertheless, even the scattered population of rural England was mainly out of Pope's reach. The lower orders of society had neither the education, the leisure nor the means to apply themselves to reading. Books were an expensive commodity. In any case, the freeholders and yeomen, a notch or two up in the social scale, were almost as unlikely to join the reading public. Shrewd in practical affairs, and capable of responding to sharply written polemics by Swift or Defoe, they had little taste for *belles lettres*.

The truth is that – despite Pope's cultivation of rustic values – his audience was aristocratic and metropolitan in colouring. He might celebrate 'the silent Shade' (*WF*, 432), but his real affinities lay in the busy city life. His real subjects were men and events, and his readership was a sophisticated, tight-knit group. If his poetry has a wider appeal today, that is not because tastes have changed but because the literary public has been greatly extended. The constituency of serious artistic interest now embraces people very different in background, occupation and income. In Pope's day, broadly speaking, it did not.

It is, then, misleading to think of Pope as a detached or culturally isolated figure. We must not confuse his elective affinities or his intellectual loyalties with his actual role as the most conspicuous man of letters in his time. Of course, Pope *professed* detachment on many occasions. His house and garden at Twickenham, on which so much care was lavished, are part of a desperate effort to camouflage a suburban life style behind a façade of agrarian repose and classic monumentalism. Similarly, his periodic 'rambles' to the provinces – never too far afield – have the air of country *retreats*: something the real countryman never needs. Pope certainly did his health some good, physically and nervously, when he visited Bath or Bevis Mount, Oxford or Down Hall. But his real staging posts were the estates of the great landowners – Stowe, Rousham, Cirencester, Hagley – where he could come as a house guest to the earls of creation. He sends back from darkest Oxfordshire a marvellous communiqué to Lady Mary Wortley Montagu (*Corr*, i, 505–8). It is one of the most brilliant letters in the English language; but it is the work of an observant tourist, and needs a trained reader to appreciate its knowing allusions and witty attitudes. Pope could be very happy for a time, deep in the provinces. So long as he had his civilized audience back home to receive his reports.

The only concrete guide to his readership is to be found in the subscription lists for his Homer. Unfortunately, no thorough social analysis of this data has yet been carried out (a task on which the present author is engaged). It is of course true that subscribers are not wholly typical of the reading public at large. They will tend to be the better-heeled, the more accessible, the less retiring among the total body of what we might call consumers. Nevertheless, it is just these factors that serve to make subscribers an influential group: opinion formers as well as readers. When Pope solicited the original two guineas entitling the subscriber to the opening instalment of the *Iliad*, he was still quite a new name to potential buyers, though already an auspicious one. With his friends he made a determined effort to drum up support, as was then normal enough. The success of the Homer venture, culminating in a profit of almost £10,000 on the two works (out of which he had to pay his collaborators on the *Odyssey*), remains a cause for wonder. Pope had managed to get some glittering names to head his list, but so did the authors of many subscription volumes. Pope's list is distinguished not by a concentration of dukes, nor by a penetration into new levels of society. He simply reached a higher proportion of the cultural élite than did his rivals, and made a more

durable impact upon them. The Homer translations became
a commercial success but they were first of all a literary triumph.

I have said that Pope's intellectual stance is not always a reliable guide to his actual relationship to society. For example,
he distanced himself politically from the London merchant class
to which his father belonged. Nevertheless, there is little doubt
that prosperous and educated members of the commercial class
were keenly aware of Pope. Again, though the law often comes
in for vigorous satire (e.g. *IH*, Sat. II, i), members of the profession were among the poet's most devoted adherents. As with
Jane Austen, Pope found a market in the very sort of people
he treated most savagely.

Conversely, Pope's expressed admirations do not imply his
acceptance by any social group as an entirety. In *The Dunciad,*
he sets off his picture of anarchic dullness with brief allusions
to tutelary figures: Swift, Chesterfield, Wyndham, Pulteney,
Murray (later the great Lord Chief Justice Mansfield), Barrow,
Atterbury. Such men are usually presented as lone warriors for
defeated causes. They stand up for values under threat from
the community at large. Characteristically, Pope endows the
forces he is opposing with power, majesty, wealth, arrogance.
By contrast, his exemplars of virtue seem frail and precarious.
A common tactic is to take the strikingly *unrepresentative* case,
perhaps in order to encourage the others: Burlington, the
untypically public-spirited peer, or Martha Blount, the least
vain of women. The natural rhetorical figure to convey this
situation is paradox:

> Great without Title, without Fortune bless'd,
> Rich ev'n when plunder'd, honour'd while oppress'd,
> Lov'd without youth, and follow'd without power,
> At home tho' exil'd, free tho' in the Tower.
>
> > (*IH*, Ep. I, i, 181–4)

By suggesting that virtue is rarely met with, Pope flatters the
reader who has recognized, and presumably endorsed, that
virtue. (Note also the oxymoron implicit in the rhyme words
blessed and *oppressed,* together with the ironic merging of *power*
and *Tower.*) It is part of his stock-in-trade to make each reader
feel that he or she is morally more acute than society at large.

A rhetorical trick of this order is necessary if Pope is to take as his victims those who will form his audience – or who are identical with such people. This means that Pope's art relies on delicate negotiation of the author–reader relationship. If he is not careful, in defining his standards he will define his own audience out of existence.

All this, let us recall, in a nation by modern standards parochial and sharply stratified. Communications were poor; the inventions of men like Abraham Darby and Thomas Newcomen (Pope's contemporaries) had not yet led to a relocation of industry. Political power was arrogated by comparatively few: it was agreed almost everywhere that the ownership of land was a sufficient title to authority in this sphere. Apart from that, a wide range of powers was given over to the local magistracy. Not merely judicial functions, but administrative and managerial tasks were cheerfully allotted to the commission of the peace. In this preindustrial situation, it would be unrealistic to look for some brash demotic art form, welding together men and women on every cultural level. There was no such thing as an eighteenth-century mass medium – pulpit oratory was perhaps the nearest the Augustans came to that. In such a world serious art is bound to be one of the territories reserved for the privileged, as one might say a game park of the spirit. There are of course chapbooks, popular woodcuts, fairground shows, but their quality is depressingly low, even if they provided a take-off board for Hogarth and Swift. It is in high art that this kind of society will express itself most adequately. And Pope – this peculiar amalgam of civic outsider and psychological insider – devoted his exceptional imaginative resources to this world. Few great writers have been as close to their immediate surroundings – its landscapes, its moods, its shouts and its murmurs. There is an eerie continuity between his audience and his subject matter, as when he dedicates to Arabella Fermor his poem about her fictional self, Belinda. To quote Maynard Mack, 'In its crowds and chandeliers and coffee spoons...it may not be the highest world that English poetry offers us, but it is the one we know best.'[5]

CHAPTER TWO

The politics of style

From his earliest years Pope set himself to introduce a new 'correctness' to English poetry. It seems an odd ambition to us; and not merely because it implies a censorious attitude towards the 'irregular' beauties of Shakespeare and Milton. Beyond all this, we are ill at ease with an aesthetic which places such a high value on what seem to us aridly technical skills. But for the Augustans it was different. The new polish they looked for in art was a matter of glamour, pride, self-confidence. 'Correct' poetry was part of a swelling nationalism and a swaggering modernism; it came ready equipped with a justification in cultural history:

> ...Britain to soft refinements less a foe,
> Wit grew polite, and Numbers learn'd to flow.
> Waller was smooth; but Dryden taught to join
> The varying verse, the full resounding line,
> The long majestic march, and energy divine.
> Tho' still some traces of our rustic vein
> And splay-foot verse, remain'd, and will remain.
> Late, very late, correctness grew our care,
> When the tir'd nation breath'd from civil war.
> Exact Racine, and Corneille's noble fire
> Show'd us that France had something to admire.
> Not but the Tragic spirit was our own,
> And full in Shakespear, fair in Otway shone:
> But Otway fail'd to polish or refine,
> And fluent Shakespear scarce effac'd a line.
> Ev'n copious Dryden, wanted or forgot,
> The last and greatest Art, the Art to blot.
>
> (*IH*, Ep. II, i, 265–81)

Note the precise distinctions drawn between Waller and Dryden, Racine and Corneille, Shakespeare and Otway. Always Pope is busy *discriminating*.

It is worth looking with some attention at the key words in this passage, especially the honorific epithets. Wit must be 'polite' – that is, civilized, courtly, free from affectation. 'Refinements' may involve the gentler qualities but can also accommodate the 'energy' of a vigorous master such as Dryden. The effects to be shunned are 'rustic', what Matthew Arnold was to characterize by his phrase 'the note of provinciality'. Instead, literature should be urbane and agreeable. The 'exact' language of the great French dramatists is commended for its classical precision and bite. One can see in all this a conscious programme, a manifesto for contemporary poets, as well as a reductive account of the sloppiness of preceding generations. There are similarities with the Imagist declaration at the start of this century, notably in the attitude of T. E. Hulme and Ezra Pound to decadent Romanticism.

This then is anything but a timid defence of arbitrary rules. It is a call to action; Pope belonged to an age group which believed itself at an important watershed in taste. In fact, some heavy demands are laid on poetry in the high Augustan era. It is permitted to relinquish the quest for false sublimity; the pressure on a major writer to produce an authentic English epic was never again to reach its Renaissance dimensions. But by way of compensation poetry was asked to mirror a social revolution. More than that, it was asked to foster and indeed guide this process. The English nation was to throw off its insularity and attain a new cosmopolitan ease. This meant that society needed a thorough course of education, and poets were to be among the principal instructors. It was no longer acceptable for writing to be crabbed, rough, ill-proportioned. But nor were the dilettante Restoration coterie-poets much help, that 'Mob of Gentlemen who wrote with Ease' (*IH*, Ep. II, i, 108). A distinct professional competence was required – a solid control masked beneath the suave insouciance of the verse.

It is easy to see how in this situation the heroic couplet acquired its overwhelming attraction. It is a shapely mode of writing, firmly structured but pleasant in appearance. It solicits a clean organization of thought; the poet must know what he wants to say first, and what second, and how he is going to get from one to the other.[1] Yet the couplet has its own aesthetic appeal, deriving from its underlying symmetry. As everyone observes, figures like parallelism and antithesis flourish strongly in the Augustan climate; somehow the ideas seem to fall into such pairings without any effort on the part of the poet. In addition, there was a definite social component in the preference for this form. Blank verse had become associated with high Miltonic aspirations. This was a view which events in Pope's lifetime did little to change. Both good poets like James Thomson in his *Seasons* (1726–30) and bad poets like Thomas Newcomb in his *Last Judgement* (1723) helped to preserve the vaunting claims of blank verse. But couplets were quite another thing. They were well bred, gentlemanly, elegant.

Let us be more concrete. Pope devoted his whole career to mastering the couplet, and we should be clear on the advantages he derived.

(1) The heroic couplet was perspicuous; it invited a lucid approach, in that the formal demands make for sequentiality.

> On this Foundation *Fame*'s high Temple stands;
> Stupendous Pile! not rear'd by mortal Hands.
> Whate'er proud *Rome,* or artful *Greece* beheld,
> Or elder *Babylon,* its Frame excell'd.
> Four Faces had the Dome, and ev'ry Face
> Of various Structure, but of equal Grace:
> Four brazen Gates, on Columns lifted high,
> Salute the diff'rent Quarters of the Sky.
> Here fabled Chiefs in darker Ages born,
> Or Worthys old, whom Arms or Arts adorn,
> Who Cities rais'd, or tam'd a monstrous Race;
> The Walls in venerable Order grace:
> Heroes in animated Marble frown,
> And Legislators seem to think in Stone.
>
> (*TF*, 61–74)

Here the ideas seem to be forming a regular queue to gain admittance to the poem. It is very different from Milton, say, where the struggle to articulate engenders a titanic struggle between thought and expression, registered in the convoluted syntax. Pope moves steadily on, like an experienced rock climber; he does not make a move until he knows where he is going after *that*.

(2) The couplet was flexible. It was in touch with conversational rhythms – indeed, Pope's later work shows an increasing tendency to adopt colloquial airs:

P. How Sir! not damn the Sharper, but the Dice?
Come on then Satire! gen'ral, unconfin'd,
Spread they broad wing, and sowze on all the Kind.
Ye Statesmen, Priests, of one Religion all!
Ye Tradesmen vile, in Army, Court or Hall!
Ye Rev'rend Atheists! – *F*[riend]. Scandal! name them, Who?
P. Why that's the thing you bid me not to do.
Who starv'd a Sister, who forswore a Debt,
I never nam'd – the Town's enquiring yet.
The pois'ning Dame – *Fr*. You mean – *P*. I don't. – *Fr*. You
     do.
P. See! now I keep the Secret, and not you.
The bribing Statesman – *Fr*. Hold! too high you go.
P. The brib'd Elector – *Fr*. There you stoop too low.
P. I fain wou'd please you, if I knew with what:
Tell me, which Knave is lawful Game, which not?

                                        (*IH*, Epilogue II, 13–27)

But such cross-talk acts are only one of innumerable effects
available to Pope. He can be high and sententious, obscene,
skittish, tender, or whatever he pleases.

(3) The form was, as it were, poetically neutral. It could
carry sustained narrative or the most delicately chiselled epitaph. Pope was able to modulate in and out of the set genres
without elaborate formal preparation – thus, *Windsor-Forest*
incorporates a topographical poem, a political panegyric, an
economic prophecy, a lyrical interlude, an Ovidian setpiece,
and much else. The poet can change gear as smoothly as he does
only because of the unassuming, inconspicuous amenity
afforded by the couplet.

(4) The couplet is particularly well adapted to a number
of rhetorical devices which suited Pope's ends. Among these
are paradox, contrived anti-climax, zeugma, syllepsis and parison. Some of these are noticeable only to the reader, a rare
one nowadays, who is trained to spot particular 'turns'. Others,
though, are very obvious – like punning. And in any case

W. K. Wimsatt has written so well on the subject that detailed
treatment is not in order here. In summary, Wimsatt shows
how in Pope 'the abstract logic of parallel and antithesis is
complicated and offset' by these other rhetorical figures, and
above all by rhyme.[2] This can be illustrated by a simple example:

> Then flash'd the living Lightning from her Eyes,
> And Screams of Horror rend th' affrighted Skies.
> Not louder Shrieks to pitying Heav'n are cast,
> When Husbands or when Lap-dogs breathe their last,   158
> Or when rich China Vessels, fall'n from high,
> In glittring Dust and painted Fragments lie!
>
> (*ROL,* III, 155–60)

Obviously the main satiric impact here comes in the second
couplet, with its delicious zeugma in line 158. But the rhyme
words enact the same confusion of levels and play the same
arch mock-heroic game. In appearance the couplet is a little
prim, which is just what the ironist asks of it.

(5) The form obliges the reader to attend carefully. There
is none of the open-ended garrulity of free verse; an analytic
hold is placed on the material even as it is enunciated. Pope
employs the heroic couplet as a placing and discriminating
device. In contemporary aesthetics, deriving from Locke and
Addison, it was usual to split the creative act between *invention*
(fancy: the synthetic power of the imagination) and *judgment*
(the operation of a critical intelligence). Particular stress was
laid on the latter, though the sturdy critic John Dennis for one
felt the emphasis was sometimes misplaced. But for Pope, as
for the Renaissance writers, concern for ordonnance was a
moral issue as well as a technical one. The poet placed his words
with minute care, rather as one would set precious stones in
a piece of fine jewellery. Precision not merely prettifies, it embodies all the intellectual commitment bestowed on the work. The
couplet, indeed, is a machine for thinking in; but it is at the
same time a jewel box, to display craftsmanship and to lend
allure to finely textured ideas:

> The lucid Squadrons round the Sails repair:
> Soft o'er the Shrouds Aerial Whispers breathe,
> That seem'd but *Zephyrs* to the Train beneath.

Some to the Sun their Insect-Wings unfold,
Waft on the Breeze, or sink in Clouds of Gold.
Transparent Forms, too fine for mortal Sight,
Their fluid Bodies half dissolv'd in Light.
Loose to the Wind their airy Garments flew,
Thin glitt'ring Textures of the filmy Dew;
Dipt in the richest Tincture of the Skies,
Where Light disports in ever-mingling Dies,
While ev'ry Beam new transient Colours flings,
Colours that change whene'er they wave their Wings.
(*ROL,* II, 56–68)

This would be exquisite writing in any context. But it is the finicky precision of the language and the minute delicacy of the verse movement that give the passage its note of intimacy. Such an impression is hard to attain with any looser-knit metrical scheme. The couplet lets us explore the tiniest detail.

Of course, not all Pope appears within the confines of a single couplet. He learnt to compose in sweeping verse paragraphs, directing the argument with measured authority. As his career went on, he became particularly adept at the larger structural devices – e.g. the resolution of a satiric poem by means of a contrasting block of compliment or celebration (often turned towards the dedicatee, as in the *Epistle to a Lady*). But it remains true that the fundamental architectural unit is not the paragraph but the couplet. Within these twenty syllables Pope deployed an extraordinary range of artifice. By ceaseless variations he defeats our expectations and avoids monotony. By small shadings of rhythm, tone or syntax he creates surprise and delight:

He look'd, and saw a sable Sorc'rer rise,
Swift to whose hand a winged volume flies:
All sudden, Gorgons hiss, and Dragons glare,
And ten-horn'd fiends and Giants rush to war.
Hell rises, Heav'n descends, and dance on Earth,
Gods, imps and monsters, music, rage and mirth,   234
A fire, a jig, a battle, and a ball,   235
Till one wide Conflagration swallows all.
(*Dun,* A, III, 229–36)

The pace quickens or slows at the poet's will (line 234 here has six stresses, line 235 only four) and there is a constant interplay between the strict metrical pattern and the free-flowing syntax, with its catalogues, suspensions, alliterative echoes and so on. For a long time, Pope was bogged down in a sterile debate concerning the relations of 'sound' and 'sense' in poetry, much of it tediously annexed to the more jejune sort of onomatopoeia. But when he devoted himself to composing, instead of theorizing, everything fell into place. Pope made the couplet into a marvellously supple piece of phonetic engineering.[3]

But it would equally be wrong to give the idea that his expressive power derives solely from the vehicle he employed. The twentieth century has been able to find in Pope almost every poetic beauty which has successively arrogated critical notice. There is plangency and lyrical grace, as in *Eloisa to Abelard*; there is vibrant metaphysical wit, as in *The Dunciad*; there is arcane symbolism, as in *The Temple of Fame*; there is myth, virtually everywhere. At present Pope is most admired for a kind of prophetic urgency, evident principally in his later works. But if teasing social badinage ever comes into fashion again, he will satisfy that demand just as easily – and much the same could be said of high moral and discursive writing. There is scarcely any aesthetic canon which would exclude Pope from literary distinction, unless it is the cult of the ill-made poem.

The wider implications of Pope's technique have never been exposed in a wholly convincing manner. In my view, his poetic style is beautifully calculated to express what might be termed (simply for convenience) the Augustan outlook on life. In the first place, it shuns obscurity, as Georgian churches sought to dissipate the gloom of Gothic structures. Second, his style operates in a consecutive manner; it nurtures logic and connection. Other poetic techniques, in other ages, have been designed to blur distinctions – to allow free movement back and forward among the constituent parts of the poem. Milton, Blake and Hopkins can all be shown to favour this mode of working. But the strength of eighteenth-century poetry was that it knew the syntactic moment to leave. Pope's verse gains momentum and verve precisely from its refusal to merge one statement into another:

> Turn then from Wits; and look on Simo's Mate,
> No Ass so meek, no Ass so obstinate;
> Or her, that owns her Faults, but never mends,
> Because she's honest, and the best of Friends:
> Or her, whose Life the Church and Scandal share,
> For ever in a Passion, or a Prayer: 106
> Or her, who laughs at Hell, but (like her Grace)
> Cries, 'Ah! how charming if there's no such place!'
> Or who in sweet vicissitude appears,
> Of Mirth and Opium, Ratafie and Tears,
> The daily Anodyne, and nightly Draught,
> To kill those foes to Fair ones, Time and Thought.
> Woman and Fool are two hard things to hit,
> For true No-meaning puzzles more than Wit.
>
> (*ME*, II, 101–14)

The successive antitheses make their point because they arrive in a prepared environment. Line 106 is full of rhetorical charge. It involves antithesis and zeugma, with a hint of paradox. The small reservation 'or a Prayer' would easily get lost in the thrashing syntax of (say) Gerard Manley Hopkins. But it springs straight out at us here, so orderly is the grammatical context.

Third, Pope's style asserts the intelligibility and connectedness of things in a genteel, elegant idiom. It manages to avoid dislocation and disruption, as the work of Pope's friend Swift did not. Again the poetic vocabulary chimes in with the prejudices of the age. As Geoffrey Tillotson, a brilliantly observant analyst of linguistic effect, once noted, 'Correctness elicits and does not abuse the reader's confidence... His alertness is intensified, his curiosity, his trust increased.'[4] Many of Pope's greatest achievements rely on this delicate negotiation with the reader; and it is crucial that Pope should get the audience on his side. Other writers in other situations can afford to alienate or insult the people whom they are addressing. Shock tactics are a common feature in modern literature. But Pope needs first

---

Ratafie a kind of cherry brandy

to enlist our sympathy. He makes writing seem a civilized business, a polite form of communication as unthreatening as (to take extreme examples) a wine list or a bus timetable. Of course, there are really the most powerful undercurrents of feeling ready to surface within the poem. But, like most of his contemporaries, Pope found a posture of innocence, a demure manner, a placid front, useful to his purposes. If his style had been less witty, polished and agreeable, he would not have been able to do many of the things he did.

Finally, Pope's style is adapted not just to contemplating or celebrating – it compares, contrasts, judges. Where other writers, before and since, have evolved a use of language which would maximize other attributes of experience, Pope was chiefly occupied by sorting and ranking functions. A comparison is needed here, in fact, to make this plain. Here is Milton's Eden:

> Thus was this place,
> A happy rural seat of various view:
> Groves whose rich Trees wept odorous Gumms and Balme,
> Others whose fruit burnisht with Golden Rinde
> Hung amiable, *Hesperian* Fables true,
> If true, here onely, and of delicious taste:
> Betwixt them Lawns, or level Downs and Flocks
> Grasing the tender herb, were interpos'd,
> Of palmie hilloc, or the flourie lap
> Of some irriguous Valley spread her store,
> Flours of all hue, and without Thorn the Rose:
> Another side, umbrageous Grots and Caves
> Of coole recess, o're which the mantling Vine
> Layes forth her purple Grape, and gently creeps
> Luxuriant; mean while murmuring waters fall
> Down the slope hills, disperst, or in a Lake,
> That to the fringed Bank with Myrtle crownd,
> Her chrystall mirror holds, unite their streams.
> The Birds thir quire apply; aires, vernal aires,
> Breathing the smell of field and grove, attune
> The trembling leaves, while Universal *Pan*
> Knit with the *Graces* and the *Hours* in dance
> Led on th' Eternal Spring.

(Paradise Lost, IV, 246–68)

Now Pope's 'Groves of Eden', transported to England, and
embodying a conscious Miltonic recollection:

> Here Hills and Vales, the Woodland and the Plain,
> Here Earth and Water seem to strive again,
> Not *Chaos*-like together crush'd and bruis'd,
> But as the World, harmoniously confus'd:
> Where Order in Variety we see,
> And where, tho' all things differ, all agree.
> Here waving Groves a chequer'd Scene display,
> And part admit and part exclude the Day;
> As some coy Nymph her Lover's warm Address
> Nor quite indulges, nor can quite repress.
> There, interspers'd in Lawns and opening Glades,
> Thin Trees arise that shun each others Shades.
> Here in full Light the russet Plains extend;
> There wrapt in Clouds the blueish Hills ascend;
> Ev'n the wild Heath displays her Purple Dies,
> And 'midst the Desart fruitful Fields arise,
> That crown'd with tufted Trees and springing Corn,
> Like verdant Isles the sable Waste adorn.
> Let *India* boast her Plants, nor envy we
> The weeping Amber or the balmy Tree,
> While by our Oaks the precious Loads are born,
> And Realms commanded which those Trees adorn.
> Not proud *Olympus* yields a nobler Sight,
> Tho' Gods assembled grace his tow'ring Height,
> Than what more humble Mountains offer here,
> Where, in their Blessings, all those Gods appear.
> See *Pan* with Flocks, with Fruits *Pomona* crown'd,
> Here blushing *Flora* paints the enamel'd Ground,
> Here *Ceres'* Gifts in waving Prospect stand,
> And nodding tempt the joyful Reaper's Hand,
> Rich Industry sits smiling on the Plains,
> And Peace and Plenty tell, a STUART reigns.
>
> (*WF*, 11–42)

Milton shows us a scene; Pope takes us on a guided tour. His
landscape is composed, planned, resonant with meanings. Milton is taken up with the sheer sensuous wonder of Eden; Pope

maps out his groves with fastidious care. He starts with a contrast on the accented '*These*' (9) and proceeds through a whole series of antitheses, explicit or implicit. Milton's 'here' is a vague locative: Pope's is set directly against a clear cut 'there'. Milton alludes for a moment to classical myth, but simply to compass his atmospheric ends – to enrich the awe and mystery. Pope applies directly to the classics, as a touchstone and contrast. His style is always quick to detect rivalries:

> While by *our* Oaks the precious Loads are born,
> And Realms commanded which *those* Trees adorn.

Pope's language is full of small direction signs, which control the relationship of one thing to another – *not/but, part/part, nor/nor, not/than*. In short, Milton presents experience, Pope arranges it. He has been shown to import into his Homer a strong emphasis on perspectives, not present in the original; and we have the same organizing process at work in *Windsor-Forest*. Pope needed a poetic language of location and comparison: and the couplet – sharp and sequential – was a key part of this language.

CHAPTER THREE

Soft numbers and good sense

These days precocity is out of favour. It makes us think of awful child prodigies and pushing mothers. But the eighteenth century could put up with primness for the sake of an emerging talent. The benefit accrued when artists like Pope and Mozart were producing in their mid teens a number of works which challenged comparison with the best adult achievement of the time. Pope's *Pastorals* came out in a volume of miscellanies in 1709, but they had been handed about in manuscript for some years previously. One of the poet's mentors, William Walsh, provided detailed criticism in response to enquiries by Pope. In this case it was not just an instinctive concern for perfection and finish which prompted such elaborate cosmetic surgery upon the text. The fact was that the *Pastorals* were deliberately intended to make Pope's name. They were a diploma piece, setting out their author's credentials to the cultivated world. In these circumstances it is perhaps surprising that Pope managed to make them aesthetically satisfying, as well as socially suitable; but he did. If he had never written another line, the *Pastorals* would show him possessed of extraordinary gifts. The refinement of their technique, the plangent melodic effects, and the sculptural beauty of the poised Arcadian scenes – all these bespeak achieved, not just promised, talent.

When the *Pastorals* were reprinted in the collective works of 1717, there was set at their head a short 'Discourse on Pastoral Poetry' dating from about 1704, when Pope was sixteen. This is a review of the extensive body of theory which had grown up around the pastoral form. As often, Pope's opinions are orthodox but first-hand. His most interesting remarks for our immediate purposes concern his statement regarding the myth of the Golden Age: 'We must therefore use some illusion to render a Pastoral delightful; and this consists in exposing only the best side of a shepherd's life, and in concealing its miseries' (TE, I, 27). In the event this does not seem to square with Pope's own practice, where there are many reminders of the limitations of the human condition. However, Pope's comments on Spenser do bear directly on his own work as a pastoralist. He points out, for example, that the device of a shepherd's calendar lends an organizing principle hitherto absent from the form: '...since by this, besides the general moral of innocence and simplicity, which is common to other authors of pastoral, [Spenser] has one peculiar to himself; he compares human Life to the several Seasons, and at once exposes to his readers a view of the great and little worlds, in their various changes and aspects' (TE, I, 32). As it turned out, the fullest imaginative development of this scheme was to be accomplished not by Pope but by his younger friend James Thomson with *The Seasons*. But the passage from the 'Discourse' is valuable because it reminds us that pastoral did not start and end for Pope with classical models. As well as Theocritus and Virgil (the latter of whom often enters Pope's text filtered through Dryden), Pope had absorbed Spenser and the early Milton – then rather *démodé* – as well as the more popular Waller.

This was appropriate, since one aim of the poems was to transport Arcady to the banks of the Thames. Joseph Warton for one thought this a little absurd: 'A mixture of British and Grecian ideas may justly be deemed a blemish,' he declared.[1] However, Pope is simply contriving one of the necessary 'illusions' or artistic fictions of the genre. The poetic effect is one of a generalized rural calm, invested with a certain languid English haziness. The sharp Mediterranean colours of classical pastoral are insensibly muted, graduated, blurred. Though there are particular antecedents for individual poems (*Spring,* Virgil's seventh eclogue; *Autumn,* the eighth, and so on), there is a conscious programme of naturalizing the form throughout. Apart from references to the Thames, Windsor, Charles II and the orders of British chivalry, Pope takes pains to celebrate the local worthy Granville, poet and statesman. The first three poems are dedicated to modern British worthies, and the last to the memory of a lady named Tempest who died, with grisly aptness, on the night of the Great Storm which convulsed the nation in 1703.

Pope also extends Spenser's seasonal plan in a number of ways. He moves from the boyish competition of *Spring* through an adolescent love plaint and a melancholy lament of deserted lovers to an elegy in *Winter* – thus creating a broad parallel between the life cycle of human beings and the course of the year. Moreover, he identifies each scene with a particular time of day: in *Spring,* it is early morning; in *Summer,* high noon; in *Autumn,* sunset; in *Winter,* midnight. The climate similarly modulates from season to season. In *Spring* the language is sweet and vernal: *Dews, fresh, fair, blushing, clear, gently, bloomy, dawning, joyous, blissful, soft, vernal, fruitful, soft* and *Sweets.* The atmosphere is caught in a single line (74):

The Sun's mild Lustre warms the vital Air.

Summer deploys a vocabulary of much more fierce and intense character: *parched, sultry, heat, panting, beams, bright, scorches, burns, fiercer, Flames. Autumn,* traditionally the season of contemplation, is filled with plangent and melancholy terms: *tender, lost, sad, deep, Murmurs, forlorn, gentle, Sighs, dye, droop, forsaken, fade, perish, mournful, spent, pains, departing.* At the end, 'the low Sun had lengthen'd ev'ry Shade' (100), an exact cameo of the poem's ebbing spirits and dispirited mood. The aural content is stronger here than elsewhere: echoes die slowly away into a vague distance. *Winter,* a formal elegy conducted by two speakers, Lycidas and Thyrsis, is redolent of dampness, chill, deprivation. Characteristic terms are *sleeping, silent, Rains, Moisture, weeping, Stream, useless, decay, gloomy, Clouds, drooping, faded, dye, dead, Flood, hapless, hollow, ceasing, neglect, refuse, shun, suspend, hush'd, Sighs, o'erflows, grief, teeming, noxious, Decay.* Several of these words are repeated, and thus reinforce the prevailing note of depression and loss – as though Nature herself were conspiring in the feeling of bereavement endured by the speakers.

In a brilliant article Georgio Melchiori has drawn attention to the presence of foreboding and mortality in the *Pastorals,* and has linked this with the iconographic tradition of '*Et in Arcadia ego*'. Melchiori makes a number of telling points, and one can well agree that the *Pastorals* 'are expressions of moods of nature all involving a twilight feeling of melancholy similar to that of Poussin's landscapes'.[2] But though death hovers over each of the poems, we should distinguish between the explicit melancholia (in the sense of humours psychology) of *Autumn* and the authentic lament of *Winter*. Nor should we overlook the buoyant animal spirits of the contest in *Spring*, where human energies are matched by the vigorous creative processes of nature; or the anarchic power of love in *Summer*, which rules mankind even when the cosmic forces are at their calmest:

> But soon the Sun with milder Rays descends
> To the cool Ocean, here his Journey ends;
> On me Love's fiercer Flames for ever prey,
> By Night he scorches, as he burns by Day.   (89–92)

As has been well said, 'what the scenery of the poems does is gather man and his concerns into the larger harmonies of Nature'. Pope finds in the conventional rhetoric of the pastoral, whether it be a singing contest or a dirge, a means of articulating man's unaltering relationship with nature. But, as at the end of *Summer*, this can take the form of feeling at odds with her. Through the stylized utterance of imaginary swains, Pope confronts the logic of existence: he poses within an emblematic landscape the great dilemmas of love and death. And in the chiselled precision of his diction he proclaims the capacity of art to endure though seasons change, men pass away and sounds die upon the air.

A kind of tailpiece to the *Pastorals* is the 'sacred Eclogue', *Messiah*, which was first published in the *Spectator* during May 1712. The poem, just over 100 lines in length, takes a number of passages from the Book of Isaiah, but it is not in any direct sense a paraphrase. Pope designed the poem as an imitation of Virgil's fourth eclogue, prophesying the birth of a child who would inaugurate a new age of justice and harmony. This eclogue had long been interpreted as a Christian allegory and virtually equated with Isaiah's foretelling of the Messiah. Pope's own biblical references are heaviest in respect of Chapters 11, 25, 35, 60 and 65 of Isaiah. The tone is consistently declamatory, excitable, even frenzied. Pope keeps everything on a high note; his imagery is rich, his movement confident, his concepts often grandiose:

> See thy bright Altars throng'd with prostrate Kings,
> And heap'd with Products of *Sabaean* Springs!

For thee, *Idume's* spicy Forests blow;
And Seeds of Gold in *Orphyr's* Mountains glow.
See Heav'n its sparkling Portals wide display,
And break upon thee in a Flood of Day!
No more the rising *Sun* shall gild the Morn,
Nor Evening *Cynthia* fill her silver Horn,
But lost, dissolv'd in thy superior Rays;
One Tyde of Glory, one unclouded Blaze,
O'erflow thy Courts...

(93–103)

It is splendidly sustained hyperbole. But one may find oneself
agreeing with R. A. Brower when he says that 'we are distracted
from the divine power to scene and to wit'.[3] Pope's delight
in violent transformations was marvellously enlisted in the third
and fourth books of *The Dunciad*. But in *Messiah* the strangeness
and magnificence of the New World envisaged outrun any
feeling of awe. The poetic temperature is so uniformly ecstatic
that we seem to be attending a banquet of the senses, rather than
sharing in a spiritual rebirth. *Messiah* remains a *tour de force*,
but it is not unfairly treated by applying that phrase to it. One
should not look in it for subtlety, any more than one expects
delicate nuances of musical texture in the 1812 Overture.

*   *   *   *   *

In many respects it is logical to proceed to *Windsor-Forest* (1713)
as the final expression of Pope's pastoral stage. And indeed
the poem is closely linked to the works we have just considered.
Most of it was written in the same early period with a triumphant
conclusion added in 1712. It deploys the familiar lexicon of
'green Retreats' and 'Shades', the idyllic landscape symbolized
by 'the Groves of *Eden*', the legends of nymph and satyr. However, *Windsor-Forest* is a great deal else. Even its strong Virgilian
colouring would be better identified as a tribute to the vein
of English Georgic recently explored by John Chalker. And this
does not exhaust the list of classical antecedents. One passage,
describing the myth of Lodona (171–218), is a conscious effort
to rival Ovid's *Metamorphoses*. There are other literary debts –
the meeting of the waters (337–48) has direct analogues in the

Faerie Queene, Book IV, in Milton's 'Vacation Exercise', *ad fin,* and in Drayton's *Poly-Olbion,* Song XVII. As elsewhere, there is a pervasive Spenserian tinge to the work which earlier commentators somehow persuaded themselves did not signify.

Beyond all this, however, there is an inclusive political-cum-patriotic theme. To read *Windsor-Forest* as a 'nature poem' – which is what the nineteenth century always did – is to guarantee disappointment. One comes up with a few beautiful lines, such as the close of the Lodona episode:

> Oft in her Glass the musing Shepherd spies
> The headlong Mountains and the downward Skies,
> The watry Landskip of the pendant Woods,
> And absent Trees that tremble in the Floods;
> In the clear azure Gleam the Flocks are seen,
> And floating Forests paint the Waves with Green.
> Thro' the fair Scene rowl slow the lingring Streams,
> Then foaming pour along, and rush into the *Thames.*
>
> (211–18)

Or again the famous section describing the dying pheasant (111–18), one of the few parts of the poem congenial to Romantic taste. But this is to mistake the central business of *Windsor-Forest.* Pope is indulging both local and national piety; he uses the forest as far more than a pastoral enclave. The clue is provided in the very first couplet:

> Thy Forests, *Windsor!* and thy green Retreats,
> At once the Monarch's and the Muse's Seats.
>
> (1–2)

That is, the district around Windsor has strong historical connections, both literary and monarchical. The basis of the 'Windsor' theme has as much to do with time as place.

It might be argued, indeed, that Pope tries to make this apposite symbol carry too much weight. Windsor performs at least seven functions within the myth developed as the poem proceeds. In the first instance, it is a royal domain; as well as the Castle, the Forest itself was a perquisite of the monarch. Second, the Forest is the site of hunting and other rapacious activities (as it happens, the events related in lines 43–92, exemplifying the cruelty of the Normans, actually concern the New Forest, but by poetic extension they are seen to belong to Windsor also). Third, the presence of the Thames is made apparent at several points. The river is celebrated as it links Windsor with the capital and the wider world; metaphorically, it is the agency through which the timber of the Forest will pass to build a new empire. Fourth, a number of earlier poets who had lived in the district are introduced into Pope's imaginative design – Surrey, Denham and Cowley among them. This also gives an opportunity to pay a fulsome compliment to Granville, the dedicatee of the poem and a minor pastoralist in his own right. Fifth, the Forest becomes something similar to Arden in *As You Like It* – a place of retirement from which to view the corruptions of the great world. In particular, Pope fixes on his elderly patron Sir William Trumbull (who had taken up residence at Easthampstead, near Pope's family home at Binfield) as an example of the happy man.

> Whom humbler Joys of home-felt Quiet please,
> Successive Study, Exercise and Ease.
>
> (239–40)

Sixth, Windsor was the centre of the orders of chivalry; and a pervasive heraldic motif is brought to a head in a passage celebrating the 'Heroes *Windsor* bore' (299–328). Finally, the natural beauty of forest and river is seen as an emblem of Edenic perfection – see the lines quoted above, p. 18.

The most important of these symbolic layers are the first and last. *Windsor-Forest* is a strongly royalist poem; it is a vehemently Stuart poem; and it is probably (though not quite conclusively) a Jacobite poem. Pope sets out to praise the recently achieved Peace of Utrecht, formally signed a month after the work was published. His choice of dedicatee is significant here, for Granville was one of the new Tory peers created to help Bolingbroke's diplomatic measures through the House of Lords. The promise of further 'Honours' to Granville (289–90) was later to be accomplished by the award of a Jacobite earldom, when Granville deserted to the Pretender's court after the Hanoverian accession. There is a good deal of hostility towards William

III in places (43 ff.: 73 ff. esp.) and though some of the more naked political animus was cut out in revisions, the poem remains implicitly anti-Hanoverian in its overall drift.

The closest analogue to *Windsor-Forest* is Sir John Denham's *Cooper's Hill,* itself a complex work with a confusing textual history. It had first been drafted prior to the Civil War in 1642, and had subsequently undergone extensive revision in the aftermath of that war. Denham incorporates a good deal of historical and constitutional reflection into his text, along with description of local events such as a stag hunt. However, the place itself is chiefly used as a convenient vantage point, from which the long-sighted Denham can pick out prominent landmarks as far distant from Egham as St Paul's Cathedral (as well as the close-at-hand Runnymede). As with the eighteenth-century 'hill-top' poets, Denham seems to need to climb to a height to get some kind of control over his material, but after this the precise locality is largely irrelevant. It is very different, as we have seen, with Pope. In *Windsor-Forest* the topography enters every corner of the poem. No longer is it a matter of a mere vantage point from which the writer can gaze out and muse on history or politics. Rather, the wider political and cultural meanings are implicit in the landscape itself. Dr Johnson's definition of local poetry has generally been applied both to *Cooper's Hill* and to *Windsor-Forest*: 'the fundamental subject is some particular landscape to be poetically described, with the addition of such embellishments as may be supplied by historical reflexion or incidental meditation'.[4] Yet there is nothing incidental about Pope's conclusions: they spring from the ongoing description of the treasures of Windsor, whether natural or wrought by men; and this running description forms almost a narrative plot as well as a ground base for the symbolism.

It has recently been discovered that Pope's own brother-in-law and nephew were taken up by the authorities for deer-stealing in the Forest just ten years after the poem appeared. There is some disagreement about his reactions to this event, and it is too early to state with confidence how Pope regarded the gradual encroachment into the area of the new Whigs and superannuated generals (one such figure was after all Lord Cobham, to whom he addressed the first of his *Moral Essays,* and

whose home at Stowe became a refuge of patriotic high-min-
dedness). It has also been suggested that Pope disapproved of
hunting in any event, and that even his mention of Anne as
a huntress (147–64) may be less admiring than has been
thought.[5] There is certainly a constant dialectic between aggres-
sion and passivity, rape and submission, which indicates Pope's
awareness of the violence acted out in the Forest even under
beneficent rule. Take the following half-submerged images of
sexual conquest:

> As some coy Nymph her Lover's Warm Address
> Nor quite indulges, nor can quite repress.   (19–20)

> Here *Ceres'* Gifts in waving Prospect stand,
> And nodding tempt the joyful Reaper's Hand.   (39–40)

> The Fields are ravish'd from th'industrious Swains.   (65)

> The Fox obscene to gaping Tombs retires.   (71)

> Whom ev'n the *Saxon* spar'd, and bloody *Dane,*
> The wanton Victims of his Sport remain.   (77–78)

> Stretch'd on the Lawn his second Hope survey,
> At once the Chaser and at once the Prey.
> Lo *Rufus* tugging at the deadly Dart,
> Bleeds in the Forest, like a wounded Hart.   (81–84)

> Still in thy Song shou'd vanquish'd *France* appear,
> And bleed for ever under *Britain's* Spear.   (310)

> Safe on my Shore each unmolested Swain
> Shall tend the Flocks, or reap the bearded Grain.   (369–70)

> There Kings shall sue, and suppliant States be seen
> Once more to bend before a *British* Queen.   (383–84)

> There purple Vengeance bath'd in Gore retires.   (417)

Along with the explicit account of the rape of Lodona, these
suggestions of molestation emphasize the fragility of the order
envisaged. As usual, the Augustan temper discerns a valuable
but precarious harmony. The subliminal effect of this imagery
is to make us wish to *defend* as well as recognize that order.

Yet in the end there is a cheerful, yea-saying patriotic air which
may be hard to accept today. Pope, like Virgil, expects to see

material expansion go hand in hand with human progress. Though history has falsified some of Pope's sanguine hopes, the vision of a new Jerusalem remains imaginatively convincing, and that is all we can ask:

> The time shall come, when free as Seas or Wind
> Unbounded *Thames* shall flow for all Mankind,
> Whole Nations enter with each swelling Tyde,
> And Seas but join the Regions they divide;
> Earth's distant Ends our Glory shall behold,
> And the new World launch forth to seek the Old.
>
> (397–402)

Perhaps it did not happen exactly like that. But Pope is not to blame. It is an ample and noble conception, registered in the dignity and unselfconscious sweep of the language. The total dream of *Windsor-Forest* is no longer, as we should say, 'viable'. But the imaginative exploration of history which nourishes that dream, and the lyrical apprehension of time and place which sustain it – these make it a deeply moving poem even in an age of disorder and feebler loyalties.

* * * * *

We must double back a couple of years, to 1711, in order to look at *An Essay on Criticism*. This interrupted the flow of pastoral-based poems with a worldly, sophisticated commentary on the present state of letters. It is a free-spoken, opinionated, devil-may-care sort of production. Ostensibly it belongs to a line of handbooks on the art of poetry inaugurated by Horace and continued by English writers of the Restoration – notably Mulgrave's *Essay upon Poetry* (1682) and Roscommon's *Essay upon Translated Verse,* together with versions of Boileau's *Art Poétique* (1674). With its high-spirited fun, however, the *Essay* seems in Pope's hands on the way towards a different genre: outright satire. The character sketches of bad critics are so maliciously damaging; the epigrams are so unconscionably bright; the fire power of the wit seems altogether to subvert the proper dignity of an 'essay'. Yet it is a deeply serious statement of aesthetic principles. And it is all the more so (puzzling as this may be

to us) because it teeters on the edge of after-dinner conversation
We feel the same unease we should experience today at finding
a Reith Lecture slotted inside a television chat show. But it is
a leading aim of the work to discountenance formalism. Pope
seeks to assimilate artistic standards within a wider code of good
breeding. He is concerned with inculcating 'true Taste' (12) in
those who are to judge literature. The concept is not purely
intellectual; it covers such things as generosity of spirit, readiness to sink small differences in a larger cause, capacity to respond readily and without prejudice. This is a lesson which
is ill adapted to a ponderous *Organon* of learning. It is rather
a branch of deportment, to be 'caught' like good manners. It
is a constitutional temper, to be displayed in everyday living
rather than locked up in libraries. It is a matter of poise, of
consideration for others, of making oneself agreeable. One
could not get much more Augustan than that.

At the centre of the undertaking lie a number of key words.
They are not, as they would be today, special neologisms, for
there was no true critical vocabulary then in existence. They
are mostly small and unsuspicious looking. A crucial term 'wit'
has been profitably explored more than once. 'Nature' has also
received scholarly attention. But there remains the expression
'Sense', often found in combinations like 'good Sense'. According to William Empson, '*Sense* is an important word, though
not used very often; but has not I think much variety of meaning
here; its function is to give a solid basis for the convolutions
of *wit* above it.' He concludes that there is 'no elaborate byplay'
surrounding the word.[6] I think that this is wrong. The term
figures twenty-four times in the text – that is, once every thirty
lines (half as often as 'wit'); and its connotations are rich and
varied. In listing these meanings we shall never have to stray
far from the core of the poem.

The term occurs first in the fourth line:

> But, of the two, less dangerous is th'Offence,
> To tire our *Patience,* than mis-lead our *Sense.*
>
> (3–4)

This rhyme sets up a characteristic opposition in terms of 'taste';
it is paralleled later by *Offence/Sense* (386–7), *Pretence/Sense*

(324–5, 578–9), *Sense/Impotence* (608–9). In each case there is a contrary notion of boorishness or affectation. The symmetry of line 4 equates 'sense' with 'patience'; the quality is thus related to temperament rather than mere cognition. Sense is often to be doubted; it should be handled with diffidence (566–7). On another occasion we are told:

> Distrustful *Sense* with modest Caution speaks.
> (626)

The humility of sense is thereby enlisted in the assault on pride (an antithesis made explicit in line 387). It is best attained through unpretentious means:

> *Horace* still charms with graceful Negligence,
> And without Method talks us into Sense.
> (653–4)

Yet the substantive qualities of true sense are imposing:

> To teach vain Wits a Science *little known,*
> T'*admire* Superior Sense, and *doubt* their own!

In these cases 'sense' might be roughly defined as equivalent to 'good sense' (which actually turns up at 25, opposed to 'false Learning', and at 524, '*Good-Nature* and *Good-Sense* must ever join', where the hyphen imports a suggestion of indissoluble union). Similar is the usage 'common Sense' (28). On one occasion the nearest equivalent might be 'horse sense':

> And none had *Sense enough to be Confuted.*
> (443)

In a number of cases the implication is rather 'intelligibility' or 'reason' as against vacuity. The contrast is often diréct:

> While their weak Heads, like Towns unfortify'd,
> 'Twixt Sense and Nonsense daily change their Side.

> Pride, where Wit fails, steps in to our Defence,
> And fills up all the *mighty Void* of *Sense*!   (209–10)

> Launch not beyon your Depth, but be discreet,
> And mark *that Point* where Sense and Dulness *meet.*   (50–1)

> But *Sense* surviv'd, when *merry Jests* were past.   (460)

Here solid sense is weighed against empty frivolity. A third group of usages offers the meaning found in an expression like, 'What is the sense of that passage?' i.e. the literal content. For instance:

> Their Praise is still – *The Stile is excellent*:
> The *Sense,* they humbly take upon Content.
>
> (307–8)

The following couplet extends this meaning towards that of 'real significance':

> *Words* are like *Leaves*; and where they most abound,
> Much *Fruit* of *Sense* beneath is rarely found.
>
> (309–10)

A further example of this strand of implication occurs at lines 116–17:

> These leave the Sense, their Learning to display,
> And those explain the Meaning quite away.

Again one sees the antithesis between true sense and meddling learning. In this category too comes the famous injunction regarding sound and sense (365).

The most interesting usages embody a wider cultural component, almost a moral ingredient one might say. In the line 'For Fools *Admire,* but Men of Sense *Approve*' (391) the opposition sets before us two versions of the critic: one enthusiastic, gushing, rapturous; the other judicious and considered, yet still warm and approbatory. Likewise with this:

> 'Tis not enough, Taste, Judgment, Learning join;
> In all you speak, let Truth and Candor shine:
> That not alone what to your *Sense* is due,
> All may allow; but seek your *Friendship* too.
>
> (562–5)

In effect, the truly sensible critic must exhibit sensibility as well as sense. And so Pope can write:

> Without *Good Breeding, Truth* is disapprov'd;
> *That* only makes *Superior* Sense *belov'd.*
>
> (576–7)

Notice the strong affective terms. 'Sense' is a solvent or a balm; it belongs to a critical intelligence made shrewd, well intentioned, hospitable to talent.

To recommend this quality Pope needs to do more than affect an easygoing gentility. He has to instil his own essay with the intimacy of familiar conversation, yet avoid a spurious urbanity which will forbid him taking sides on important matters. Actually, the poem is often mischievous, if not catty:

> In the fat Age of Pleasure, Wealth, and Ease,
> Sprung the rank Weed, and thriv'd with large Increase;
> When *Love* was all an easie Monarch's Care;
> Seldom at *Council,* never in a *War*:
> *Jilts* rul'd the State, and Statesmen *Farces* writ;
> Nay *Wits* had *Pensions, and young Lords had Wit*:
> The Fair sate panting at a *Courtier's Play.*
> And not a Mask went *unimprov'd* away.

(534–41)

Manners, as Pope understands them, extend beyond mere deference to everything and everybody. They involve a lively discrimination of good and bad; but they rule out captious or niggling criticism. The ideal is a humorous, tolerant but perceptive approach to books and men. It means recognizing the genuinely great (as Homer), not for form's sake but as a commitment to the lastingly good. It permits dissent from the lazy orthodoxies or outworn pieties. And it discourages temporizing:

> With mean Complacence ne'er betray your Trust,
> Nor be so *Civil* as to prove *Unjust*;
> Fear not the Anger of the Wise to raise;
> Those best can *bear Reproof,* who *merit Praise.*

(580–3)

The *Essay* is divided into three main parts. The first section sets out the ideal order of nature, as shown to us by the ancients, and the way in which criticism can support great literature, rather than hinder it. The second section considers the obstacles to-

---

an easie Monarch Charles II

wards attaining this ideal, and anatomizes the faults then most in evidence in critical practice. The final part outlines a plan for reformation, by which true taste may again prevail. This culminates in a broad historical account of the progress of criticism, isolating a number of models ancient and modern. Within each section, though the development of ideas sentence by sentence is clear enough, there is no very tight argumentative scheme. And the table of contents set at the head of the poem (which may not be Pope's own) certainly exaggerates its logical coherence. But it is worth repeating that Pope had in mind not a regular system, a new code of 'rules', but a cultivated discourse in which certain habits of mind should be encouraged and others discountenanced. To appreciate his purposes, we must train ourselves not to read for detached maxims or discrete *pensées* – striking as the individual lines often are. Instead, we must come to the poem with our aesthetic faculties sharpened, as though we were listening to a rhetorical concerto, full of brilliant cadenzas, built around contrasts of form and phrasing, shifting nimbly in timbre and register but always melodious and agreeable. Anyone who thinks that a serious treatment of critical problems must involve crabbed jargon or graceless clatter need only turn to Pope's *Essay*. The performance is lively, the accents are genial, and the overall effect thoroughly well tempered. It is a pity our own criticism is so rarely any of these things.

CHAPTER FOUR

✳ Fancy's maze

Pope's most perfect achievement is also in some ways his most fanciful creation. *The Rape of the Lock* first appeared in two cantos, running to 142 and 192 lines respectively. This was in a miscellany published by the bookseller Bernard Lintot in May 1712. Composition probably goes back to the previous autumn, when Pope was asked by his friend John Caryll to pour some oil on a family quarrel. The details are somewhat mysterious. We know only that Robert, seventh Lord Petre, had snipped off a lock of hair from the head of Miss Arabella Fermor. Arabella came from a long-established Catholic family, like Lord Petre. She had been bred in a French convent, and was well known as a society 'toast'. We cannot be certain how serious the relationship between the two young people (both in their early twenties) had been. But if it was formerly close, it soon broke down without any help or hindrance from Pope. Lord Petre married a Lancashire heiress two months before the first version of the *Rape* was published. A year later, still only twenty-three, he died of smallpox. Shortly afterwards Arabella married a Berkshire squire. She lived in a quiet and anonymous life until her death in 1738.

These bare bones of anecdote, miraculously, Pope clothed with a rich and compelling fiction. He knew the principals very slightly, if at all; he had, it is safe to say, not witnessed anything of the original event; and he had scarcely any more reason to care about the junketings of the Augustan *jeunesse dorée* than we have today. He was excluded from such high life frivolities by birth, ill health and perhaps inclination. When Caryll asked him, then, to 'make a jest of it, and laugh them together again', it was his literary instincts that were roused, not strong personal concern. This is particularly evident in the revised version, the one we read today. Pope expanded the poem into five cantos during the latter part of 1713, and the new work – now two and a half times its original size – came out in March 1714. It was received with warm acclaim, and (a rarer thing) it has continued to justify the taste of the time.

The longer version is subtitled 'an heroi-comical poem'. Usually this is translated as 'mock-heroic', and though a technical distinction can be drawn this will do well enough. Mock-heroic was one of a number of Augustan forms which threw violently together two disparate value systems. Like burlesque, 'imitation' and the so-called town pastoral, it served to juxtapose seemingly irreconcilable ideas. In this particular case, Pope manages to invoke through his diction and certain structural episodes the world of epic – i.e. a mode associated with grandeur, suggesting the antique, masculine, serious and martial aspects of experience. The subject matter is 'slight', however, as we are told at the outset (*ROL,* I, 5). We are presented with modern life from a feminine viewpoint, comically observed and domestic rather than heroic in compass. The trick is to make the epic scale of things point up the triviality of contemporary society, without itself getting sullied by the contact. Pope was then embarking on his translation of Homer, and indeed there are some curious verbal analogues between the *Rape* and his own rendition of the *Iliad.* So it is not to be expected that Pope will allow the epic to emerge in a mangled condition. What he is after might be looked on as a sort of extended paradox. A small affair is ridiculed by a staged confrontation with more weighty matters; but in the process it may also be irradiated and transformed.

It seems clear that Pope's chief aim was to take up an excellent poetic opportunity. He must have known that his poem, even when it circulated only in manuscript, was calculated to stir things up rather than to heal the breach. Arabella herself, after indulging her vanity for a while, decided she did not like the *Rape.* Pope thereupon composed a marvellously double-edged dedication, which contains some of the complexity of attitude found in the poem proper. Without any grossness Pope manages to reassure Arabella that the poem *is* a compliment to her and yet to reinforce many of the satiric innuendos found in the text: 'As to the following Canto's, all the Passages of them are as Fabulous, as the Vision at the Beginning, or the Transformation at the End; (except the Loss of your Hair, which I always mention with Reverence).' It is certainly true that Belinda does receive a proud apotheosis at the conclusion, and one can understand a girl of Arabella's background feeling a little confused about it all. The final paragraph of the poem, ironic as it may appear, contains a literal truth: the notion that when 'yourself shall die', there will be immortality through the verse:

> *This Lock,* the Muse shall consecrate to Fame,
> And mid'st the Stars inscribe *Belinda's* Name!
>
> (V, 149–50)

This is a fine couplet to go out on, but it happens to be accurate. This poem, the *Lock,* has given posterior fame to an unimportant girl who would otherwise be totally lost to history. As it is, we can scarcely scrape together a real-life biography for Arabella: untimely fires, Dickensian law suits and mutilated parish registers have made research all but impossible. But Belinda lives on, as the poem promises she will.

Until recently it was customary to read the poem as a brilliant bit of nothing. If substance was granted to the *Rape* at all, then this was identified with 'social satire'. A different attitude now prevails, and without undue complacence one can welcome this as a more intelligent and inclusive approach to the imaginative workings of the poem. We see with growing clarity that the *Rape* is not just a slap in the face for frivolous socialites. It is also on one level an Ovidian myth, a story of magical transformations. Again, it has been read as 'a fantasy of enchantment', which blends native faery lore with Rosicrucian philosophy.[1] In a word, the supernatural has taken its place alongside the worldly in our view of the poem, and the psychic space it occupies. One wouldn't be surprised to see elements of freemasonry detected one of these days.

All this is much to the good. But it would be wrong to forget other strands in the work, less ethereal in their nature. The *Rape* keeps up a constant flow of *risqué* allusions to sex, and of course the title itself makes one such *double entendre.* There is a profoundly physical, even biological, cast to many areas of the text. This is particularly apparent in the sections involving the gnomes, who represent the repressed, hoarding mentality of prudes as against the 'light' (sexually irresponsible) troop of sylphs. Here Pope has devised a symbol of extraordinarily rich poetic implication. Of all the additions he made in the second version, which include the entire mythology of sylphs

and gnomes, it is the Cave of Spleen at the start of Canto IV
which best reveals Pope's capacity to pack dense human implication into fantastic visions. The materials are those of
abnormal psychology; the container, so to speak, is surrealist
imagery. The 'dusky melancholy Spright' Umbriel descends to
a horrific underworld grotto, 'sheltered close from Air'. Here
resides Spleen, the source of female affectation, breeder of hysteria and wild delusions, 'Parent' both of paranoia and of the
creative urge. Probably 'spleen' is a euphemism for the womb –
at least, the disorders rampant in the Cave are all strongly
inclined towards sexual and procreative functions:

> Unnumber'd Throngs on ev'ry side are seen
> Of Bodies chang'd to various Forms by *Spleen*.
> Here living *Teapots* stand, one Arm held out,
> One bent; the Handle this, and that the Spout:
> A Pipkin there like *Homer's Tripod* walks;
> Here sighs a Jar, and there a Goose-pye talks;
> Men prove with Child, as pow'rful Fancy works,
> And Maids turn'd Bottels, call aloud for Corks.
>
> (IV, 47–54)

This is more than a grotesque episode outside the main action.
The goddess Spleen gives Umbriel 'a wondrous Bag' and a vial
containing female sighs and tears. On reaching the upper world
he comes on Belinda in the arms of the disagreeable Thalestris:

> Full o'er their Heads the swelling Bag he rent,
> And all the Furies issued at the Vent.
>
> (IV, 91–2)

Subsequently he discharges the vial also (IV, 141). Hence comes
the triumph of hysteria and neurosis acted out in the contests
of Canto V.

Many readers, of course, will respond more immediately to
the glittering description of the toilet at the end of the first
Canto, or the ravishing picture of the sylphs in the second.
In its delicacy and precision the poetry mimics the feminine
postures which the epic has been forced to adopt. Similarly,
the slightly barbaric symbolism of playing cards is beautifully
caught in language of self-deflating pomposity – one is

reminded by the diction that these are no Homeric warriors
but mere paper tigers from the toy cupboard:

> Ev'n mighty *Pam* that Kings and Queens o'erthrew,
> And mow'd down Armies in the Fights of *Lu,*
> Sad Chance of War! now, destitute of Aid,
> Falls undistinguish'd by the Victor *Spade*!
> Thus far both Armies to *Belinda* yield;
> Now to the *Baron* Fate inclines the Field.
> His warlike *Amazon* her Host invades,
> Th' Imperial Consort of the Crown of *Spades*.
> The *Club's* black Tyrant first her Victim dy'd,
> Spite of his haughty Mien, and barb'rous Pride:
> What boots the Regal Circle on his Head,
> His Giant Limbs in State unwieldy spread?
>
> (III, 61–72)

These are the games that lovers play when in reality (as the
visit to the Cave of Spleen shows us) their underlying desires
are to treat in more directly carnal ways. Belinda's code, of
course, prevents her admitting this. Her outrage at the Baron's
assault is all the greater because it represents what subcon-
sciously she has been wishing for and inviting all along.

There is an even finer example of the accord between satiric
purpose and verbal texture later in the same canto. This comes
with the appearance of the coffee, announced with all the stateli-
ness of a professional toast-master:

> For lo! the Board with Cups and Spoons is crown'd,
> The Berries crackle, and the Mill turns round.
> On shining Altars of *Japan* they raise
> The silver Lamp; the fiery Spirits blaze.
> From silver Spouts the grateful Liquors glide,
> While *China's* Earth receives the smoking Tyde.
> At once they gratify their Scent and Taste,
> And frequent Cups prolong the rich Repast.   112
> Strait hover round the Fair her Airy Band;
> Some, as she sip'd, the fuming Liquor fann'd,
> Some, o'er her Lap their careful Plumes display'd,
> Trembling, and conscious of the rich Brocade.
>
> (III, 105–16)

Pope satirizes the coffee ritual in itself, but he also keeps his eye closely on the appliances used. As often in the poem, the mysterious East is present only as a provider of luxury goods; the diction takes on a heavy, burnished effect like that of the lacquered utensils. The sylphs turn napkins as the whole verse minces and teeters around. There is an extraordinary evocation of fragrance, allied to a keen sense of pointlessness – the flat movement of line 112 suggests time being killed. And of course there is the usual vague foreboding – the participants dread a cup being spilt, a dress being marked, a pot being broken. Standing outside the action, we (and the poet) await a more dire offence.

One effect of Pope's stylistic manoeuvres is to give us an impression of closeness, intimacy, warmth. The great outside world is readily shut out. Everything is on a small scale; in surveying the toilet our eyes are required to make only tiny movements as we pick up one detail after another. Much of the imagery is tactile, suggesting not just the gauzy femininity of the fabrics but also the constant availability of nice material things. The objects are pleasant to the touch, and we always have enough time to handle them and appreciate the fine workmanship that has gone into them. In this, Belinda's world is like Pope's poem. He too has lavished artistry and delicate handicraft on the thing he has produced. In making us attend closely to the domestic furniture, Pope gives us a superb picture of emptily gracious living. But he forces us to observe the comparable skill of his own minute rendition. And here, it may be, difficulties in response begin for some readers.

The problem had better be faced in its most acute form. This arises in the criticism that Pope, instead of excoriating Belinda and her whole milieu, stays to worship her. On this account, the poem – though officially satiric, and presumably destructive – betrays an increasing willingness to accept Belinda's pseudo-divine status as something pleasant to contemplate imaginatively, if not believable *tout court*. I think there is something in this line of argument, but it is not clear how damaging it is to the artistic standing of the *Rape*. For Pope is not obliged *qua* satirist to hate anybody, let alone everybody; he has, like any other writer, to present a coherent and intelligible view

[marginal note, handwritten: Creates world in miniature]

of his subject. The satirist looks at life under one particular
aspect, seeking the follies and affectations which stand in viola-
tion of good sense or taste. But it is possible to condemn the
sin and love the sinner; and Belinda after all is rather sumptuous
through her silliness and vanity, not in spite of them. Pope lets
us know in a hundred ways that she *is* silly, but he responds
aesthetically to her elaborate self-projection. Her 'awful Beauty'
takes an awful lot of putting on, and we witness every last dab
of the power puff. But the effect in the end is distinctly pleasant,
and the poetry acknowledges as much. Transferred to the moral
sphere, we may say that Pope can bring out the shallowness of
Belinda's round, and the inadequacy of her code, without losing
the capacity to enjoy its brittle amusements or understand its
enticements to an impressionable girl. And the ending allows
Belinda, as we have seen, a kind of consolation. I agree with
the critic who has said that Pope 'rises above [Clarissa's] almost
tragic view to a triumphant declaration of the power that beauty,
for all its moral flimsiness, brings to a battle against mutability'.[2]

It need not surprise us that Pope can endorse, on one level,
a divinity that is proffered on another in purely joking fashion.
The Rape of the Lock operates primarily through laughter and
acceptance. Its rich veins of fantasy reach some strange areas
of consciousness, but they are not disturbing in the last analysis,
because the controlling vision is comic. That is to say, the imaginative delight of contemplating the disorder and arranging
it into poetic order is still greater than the distress undergone.
At this stage not only can Pope make sense of things; he can
take joy in doing so, and convey that to us in the fabric of
the poem.

*   *   *   *   *

The Rape of the Lock has never lacked admirers. But another poem
of this period, *The Temple of Fame* (1715), has only recently
acquired a secure place of eminence within Pope's canon.
Indeed, it was not until G. Wilson Knight produced a reading
of the poem in 1955 that serious attention was devoted to the
poem.[3] Even now the critical heritage is a slender one; the bur-
geoning anthologies of work on Pope contain little by way of
comment on *The Temple of Fame*. Composition probably goes

back to 1711 or thereabouts, with later revisions. Pope's model, freely adapted, was *The House of Fame*, a poem in three books left unfinished by Chaucer after he had completed some 2000 lines. Pope compresses the work into 524 lines by a variety of means. He concentrates on the material presented in Chaucer's third book for the most part, leaving out the temple of Venus and the airborne journey to the house of Rumour. In fact, the medieval vision soon modulates in Pope to a survey of fame, as the Renaissance understood it, and to heroic exemplars drawn chiefly from the writings of Sir William Temple. 'Indeed,' says Tillotson, 'the *Temple of Fame* may be regarded as a document in the controversy of the ancient and moderns',[4] that curious cultural debate which divided Europe during Pope's formative years. If so, the poem is unambiguously on the side of the ancients, like Swift's *Battle of the Books* (1704). As usual, Pope employs an emblem already developed by previous artists: quite apart from previous treatments in poetry and essays, there had been a temple of Fame in one of Ben Jonson's masques, designed by Inigo Jones. The architecture of Pope's structure resembles the theatrical baroque of Vanbrugh and Hawksmoor more than it does the chaste Palladian style of Inigo Jones. But by this time Palladianism was already developing associations with Whiggery.

But the interest of the poem lies not so much in its manipulation of traditional themes (whether derived from Chaucer, the Renaissance humanists, or the Ancients and Moderns) as in its personal meaning – an inner logic based on Pope's especially acute feelings for the artistic vocation. It is possible to describe the working method as 'symbolic', as Wilson Knight does. There is certainly a direct line, as has often been noted, to the evocation of the 'Temple of Infamy' in *The Dunciad* (*Dun,* IV, 319, note). Nevertheless, the older term 'allegory' seems to me more accurate. Pope has found in the description of the temple and its decorative motifs not just a symbol of the artistic condition (the glory he craved; the envy he must face; the idiocies of fashionable chat) but also a moral metaphor – which is what allegory is. The dream framework allows Pope to register through scene painting and description his sense of 'the burden of the past' and of the challenge it posed to his poetic identity.

He was, all his life, strongly drawn towards a vein of serious fantasy. If that expression is not very clear, its drift should emerge from this letter which Pope wrote to a woman friend in 1723:

> This beautiful season will raise up so many Rural Images & Descriptions in a Poetical Mind that I expect You & all such as you (if there be any such), at least all who are not Downright dull Translators like your Servant, must necessarily be productive of Verses. I lately saw a sketch on this way on the Bower of Bedington. I could wish you tryd something in the descriptive way on any Subject you please, mixd with Vision & Moral; like the Pieces of the old Provençal Poets, which abound with Fancy & are the most amusing scenes in nature. There are 3 or 4 of this kind in Chaucer admirable: The Flower & the Leaf every body has been delighted with. I have long had an inclination to tell a Fairy tale; the more wild & exotic the better, therefore a *Vision,* which is confined to no rules of probability, will take in all the Variety & luxuriancy of Description you will. Provided there be an apparent moral to it. I think one or 2 of the Persian Tales would give one Hints for such an Invention: And perhaps if the Scenes were taken from Real places that are known, in order to compliment particular Gardens & Buildings of a fine Taste, (as I believe several of Chaucer's descriptions do, tho tis what nobody has observd) it would add great beauty to the whole.
>
> (*Corr,* ii, 202–3)

Pope concludes by undertaking 'to find a Tale that shoud bring [the descriptions] all together: which you'l think an odd undertaking, but in a Piece of this fanciful & Imaginary nature I am sure is practicable'. *The Temple of Fame,* in fact, was itself an 'odd undertaking' of a comparable scope, though slightly different direction.

The structure looks more awkward than it really is. The poet spends less time than his medieval counterpart in outlining the circumstances of the dream. He launches us almost immediately into a glittering 'prospect' such as the Augustans loved to contemplate. Dominating the scene stands the towering mass which is Fame's palace, perched on a rock of dazzlingly pure ice. The

structure itself is regular but not symmetrical; each face is fes-
tooned with allegorical figures representing different orders of
civilization. The language is dense with rich and jewelled effects,
but this is far from an empty aureate diction. Every speck of
gilding has its allegorical point:

> Of *Gothic* Structure was the Northern Side,
> O'er-wrought with Ornaments of barb'rous Pride.
> There huge Colosses rose, with Trophies crown'd,
> And *Runic* Characters were grav'd around:
> There sate *Zamolxis* with erected Eyes,
> And *Odin* here in mimick Trances dies.
> There, on rude Iron Columns smear'd with Blood,
> The horrid Forms of *Scythian* Heroes stood,
> *Druids* and *Bards* (their once loud Harps unstrung)
> And Youths that dy'd to be by Poets sung.
> These and a Thousand more of doubtful Fame,
> To whom old Fables gave a lasting Name,
> In Ranks adorn'd the Temple's outward Face;
> The Wall in Lustre and Effect like Glass,
> Which o'er each Object casting various Dies,
> Enlarges some, and others multiplies.
>
> (119–34)

The trick is to make architectural and archaeological remains
'freeze' a given culture in its characteristic posture: 'Heroes
in animated Marble frown, / And Legislators seem to think in
Stone' (73–4). At the centre of the edifice stand effigies of the
greatest among ancients – Homer, Virgil, Pindar, Horace, Aristotle and Cicero. There follows a description of Fame herself,
rendered in Pope's most vivid primary colours, and then the
summoning (as later in *The Dunciad*) of all supplicants to the
goddess. She arbitrates between the various claims of scholars,
virtuous livers, military adventurers, debs' delights, politicians
and others. The style at this point takes on a lighter air, and
the air of busy comedy is reinforced by the raucous blasts of
Fame's trumpet that burst forth at intervals.

Suddenly, with the surreal disconnectedness of a dream, the
levée vanishes and the poet finds himself in a different place,
identified as the Temple of Rumour. An extraordinary passage

of eddying sounds follows, introducing the description of what
we might call today the publicity machine. Pope's verse beautifully catches the Babel of conflicting reports, 'All neither wholly
false, nor wholly true' (456). After this vision – or rather evocation, for it is primarily aural – of the global village of rumour,
the poet himself presents his candidacy to Fame. With becoming
modesty, he expresses a desire for honest fame, not bought
at the expense of others. The passage forms a kind of personal
tailpiece to the work – as in *Windsor-Forest* the most directly
expressive writing comes at the end. Nevertheless, it is the central
portion of *The Temple of Fame* that most fully articulates Pope's
view of art as an imperishable medium of human expression.
It is what the dreamer perceives, not what he utters, which lies
at the heart of the allegory. The first duty of the imagination
is not to transform, still less to comment: it is to apprehend.
Pope was the last great poet who could confront his own destiny
through allegorical description as well as through personal con-
fession.

*　*　*　*　*

In 1717 Pope reached the pinnacle of his early fame with a
splendid edition of his *Works,* issued in folio and in quarto,
and providing a canonical restatement of his achievements to
date – something in the manner of a painter's 'retrospective'
exhibition today. He also wrote an intelligent and pleasantly
ironic preface.[5] But along with the established favourites, Pope
printed for the first time a number of impressive (though mainly
short) poems. These include the delightful verses 'To a Young
Lady on her Leaving the Town after the Coronation', one of
his most piquant blends of romantic feeling and cynicism. However, it was two exercises in the fashionable Ovidian style that
excited the greatest interest: *Eloisa to Abelard* and the *Elegy to
the Memory of an Unfortunate Lady.* For several generations these
were among Pope's most widely appreciated works, especially
with women readers.

Set conspicuously at the end of the volume, *Eloisa to Abelard*
is the longer and more complex. It is a heroic epistle – that
is to say, a dramatized expression of a lover's feelings, conveyed
through an address to the absent loved one. The origin is the

series of *Heroides* written by Ovid, with a limited number of classical analogues. The form had been widely practised during the Renaissance, with Drayton's work *Englands Heroicall Epistles*, written at the end of the seventeenth century, a distinguished example. A fresh vogue broke out around 1700; Drayton was adapted to modern taste, and a prose equivalent was developed with the letters of a Portuguese nun in the 1670s. In 1713 the poet and musician John Hughes, whom Pope knew quite well, brought out a translation of the letters of Abelard and Heloise. This soon came to be regarded as the definitive story of its kind. The twelfth-century scholar Abelard had contracted a liaison with an eighteen-year-old girl, who had borne his child. When the affair came to light Heloise was forced to enter a nunnery and Abelard was castrated by a gang of hired ruffians. The supposed letters date from a few years later, when Abelard had founded the monastery of the Paraclete. Hughes's version from the French was the direct spur to Pope, who probably began the poem not long after its appearance.

But Pope does much more than versify Hughes. He was a Roman Catholic, as Hughes was not, and this colours the entire poem. Moreover, he was in closer touch with the original *Heroides* than were most of the fashionable makers of heroic epistles. It is true that Pope saw antiquity through the filter of the Renaissance, much as Ravel saw the ancient world through an eighteenth-century reflector. But though he had more recent authors in his consciousness (Crashaw, Dryden, Milton), he had worked directly on the text of Ovid when translating one epistle for a collection published in 1712. More widely, it can be said that Pope felt more personal commitment to the form than many of those with which he had been experimenting. On one level, it permitted him to express a decorous longing for Lady Mary Wortley Montagu, then in Constantinople, and still the object of a deep attachment. In addition, it was a genre with fewer stylistic prescriptions than most. Pope could display a whole range of moods in a short space, and with his urge towards a kind of organic virtuosity this was just what he wanted.

The poem that emerges is vivid, highly volatile and yet (some would think, surprisingly) altogether Augustan. The successive

movements of Eloisa's heart are charted with a precision possible only to an accomplished rhetorician. Eloisa utters a series
of conflicting hopes and fears, each registered appropriately
in the shifting textures of the verse. The immediacy of the form
is proclaimed:

> Heav'n first taught letters for some wretch's aid,
> Some banish'd lover, or some captive maid;
> They live, they speak, they breathe what love inspires,
> Warm from the soul, and faithful to its fires,
> The virgin's wish without her fears impart,
> Excuse the blush, and pour out all her heart,
> Speed the soft intercourse from soul to soul,
> And waft a sigh from *Indus* to the *Pole*.
>
> (51–8)

Sometimes the poem assumes the guise of an erotic lyric; at
others, a Gothic nightpiece; sometimes the contradictory
impulses within 'this rebellious heart' are allowed direct expression, and then again they are symbolized in atmospheric landscape or the hyper-intense vision of dreams:

> ...Methinks we wandring go
> Thro' dreary wastes, and weep each other's woe;
> Where round some mould'ring tow'r pale ivy creeps,
> And low-brow'd rocks hang nodding o'er the deeps.
> Sudden you mount! you beckon from the skies;
> Clouds interpose, waves roar, and winds arise.
> I shriek, start up, the same sad prospect find,
> And wake to all the griefs I left behind.
>
> (241–8)

The great imaginative power of *Eloisa to Abelard* derives from the
skill with which Pope tailors his rhetoric to suit the psychological needs of the epistle. His poem marvellously renders the
tumult of feelings within Eloisa; the subtlest modulations in
sound and sense are used to colour in gradations of emotion.

Even more histrionic in technique is the *Elegy*, devoted to
the memory of an unnamed woman who had killed herself,
presumably as the result of frustrated love. An almost feverish
quality at the start is broken into by metaphysical speculations,

an imprecation direction against the woman's 'false guardian',
and a flash of Pope's best satiric manner:

> What tho' no friends in sable weeds appear,
> Grieve for an hour, perhaps, then mourn a year,
> And bear about the mockery of woe
> To midnight dances, and the publick show?
> What tho' no weeping Loves thy ashes grace,
> Nor polish'd marble emulate thy face?
> What tho' no sacred earth allow thee room,
> Nor hallow'd dirge be mutter'd o'er thy tomb?
>
> (55–62)

There is just enough animus in that word *mutter'd* to jolt us
for a moment. And when Pope passes on to a studied epitaph
(later set to music and published in a catch-book) we expect
the poem to end on a note of lapidary eloquence:

> A heap of dust alone remains of thee;
> 'Tis all thou art, and all the proud shall be!
>
> (73–4)

But there is a short postlude, suggesting that even the elegy-
maker will some day need his own elegy – a thought apt also
in the case of Gray's famous poem. There is the merest suspicion
in this ending that Pope is threatening Lady Mary that he, too,
will die with his love unrequited, and that she ought to satisfy
his passion before it is too late. Such feelings are deeply buried
beneath the conventional folds of the language, but it is hard
to feel they are not there.

Pope had now reached a turning point in his career. The
1717 volume not only contained his best poems to that date;
it included almost all his substantial 'original' works prior to
the first version of *The Dunciad*. His main activities for the next
decade were to lie in the margins of creative writing – translating Homer, editing Shakespeare, parodying the wits in Scriblerian farce. The maze of fancy was now about to dissolve.

CHAPTER FIVE

Homer and Shakespeare

Pope's Homer is no longer a current classic. But that has little to do with Pope or Homer — it is a limiting fact about ourselves. From his early years Pope had been fascinated by the large illustrated translation of Homer, put out by John Ogilby (1660–9). This was a storehouse of legend and narrative, which not even Ogilby's ponderous couplets could render less than entrancing to a poetry-struck boy. Later Pope came to know equally well a more distinguished version: the famous *Iliad* (in fourteeners) and *Odyssey* of George Chapman (1598–1615). His own annotated copy of Chapman survives. Apart from these, there was a complete English translation by the philosopher Thomas Hobbes (1676–7) and a French prose version by the classical scholar Anne Dacier, from which the *Iliad* had been turned into English by a composite team including William Broome (1712). Several shorter portions of Homer had been translated, normally a book at a time. Of these the most important were Dryden's *Iliad,* Book i, in his *Fables Ancient and Modern* (1700), and Pope's own rendering of an episode from the *Iliad,* published in Tonson's *Miscellanies* (1709).

It is evident that Pope came to his work around 1713 with his head suffused by the ambition to outdo all his predecessors.[1] His original poems of this period – the *Rape* especially, but also *Windsor-Forest* and the *Temple of Fame* – show him perfecting his diction and, so to speak, retooling for the task. He managed to attract a body of subscribers that was not just large in number (though not outstandingly vast) but truly eminent in social and cultural terms. Moreover, he struck a good bargain with the publisher Bernard Lintot, who in a sense paid for the privilege of acting as Pope's handling agent. The *Iliad* appeared in six volumes between June 1715 and May 1720. Initially it had to compete with a rival translation put out by a member of Addison's circle named Thomas Tickell. But before long even Oxford had abandoned this lost cause, and acknowledged Pope the better man. Henceforth he could go on in splendid isolation.

When the *Iliad* was completed he turned with only a brief pause to the *Odyssey*. Tiring of the lonely burden, he engaged two minor Cambridge poets, Elijah Fenton and William Broome, to assist with the task. Broome, the better attuned of the two to epic, undertook eight books (II, VI, VIII, XI, XII, XVI, XVIII and XXIII), Fenton four only (I, IV, XIX and XX). Pope took the remaining twelve and revised his collaborators' share with a good deal of solicitude. Initially he attempted to keep this labour-sharing device a secret. But the truth gradually seeped out, and in due course Pope was forced to admit it, gracelessly it must be said. The *Odyssey* appeared in 1725–6, by which time Pope was already back in personal contact with Swift, and itching to return to satire.

But it would be altogether wrong to suppose that Pope had deserted 'creative' writing when he applied himself to Homer. In the first place, he was satisfying a deep urge which European poets had felt since the early Renaissance, to create a modern epic. Of course, this was not ordinarily understood to mean translating an ancient epic, and Pope himself hankered after a true British *Brutiad*. But in the event Pope did write the classic Augustan poem, for all his fussy determination to show himself a scholar. Though he contrasted himself unfavourably with his friend Parnell ('I a Hackney Scribler, You a Grecian & bred at a University, I a poor Englishman of my own Educating', *Corr,* i, 226), there is no doubt this represents his habitual mock modesty. He made great efforts to familiarize himself with all the essential material. As well as the text and the earlier translations, he studied a large number of commentators. The more important of these were Archbishop Eustathius, whose work he had specially digested, and Madame Dacier. His intention was to support Madame Dacier against those who had taken the Moderns' side in opposition to the Ancients, during that celebrated but unfathomable quarrel of the late seventeenth century. She regarded him as an embarrassing ally, and disavowed Pope. But he remained loyal to his position, stoutly insisting on the supremacy of Homer over all other poets. And whilst he never became a technical scholar of high distinction, he had Greek enough to feel his way into the spirit, as well as convey the letter, of Homer. He strove to be accurate, but this was a necessary condition for success, not a sufficient one. His aim was to get hold of the central energy in the Greek poet, that '*vivida vis animi*' which placed him above the formally competent or historically interesting survivors of the ancient world.

Primarily this was a matter of finding an appropriate style. It has been well said that 'Pope's accomplishment with Homer is remarkable for its irradiation of poetry by poetry' (TE, VII, clxxxvii). His own diction and metric could not directly mimic Homer's, but he evolved an English style comparable in lift, surge and propulsion, and equal to the most exalted tasks which the Greek imposed on it. This meant taking stylistic risks: 'He crams his lines with every imaginable variety of rhetorical excitement. Lexical and syntactic dullness seems to him the worst of insults to the poet he is translating' (TE, VII, clxxxi). The result is a poem with huge innate dignity, which never knowingly undersells Homer – when Pope fails, he fails on the high side of his author. There is none of the burlesque or travesty found in some seventeenth-century versions, which summon up the world of the Hogarth print, 'Strolling Actresses Dressing in a Barn'. Pope's gods are godlike, and his verse is always striving to meet Homer at the level of his most elevated inspiration.

Pope admired in Homer 'that noble simplicity' (*Corr,* i, 44) which yet went with 'very Copious' diction. It is part of the translator's task, he tells us in the Preface, to follow 'modestly in [Homer's] Footsteps':

> Where his Diction is bold and lofty, let us raise ours as high as we can; but where his is plain and humble, we ought not to be deterr'd from imitating him by the fear of incurring the Censure of a meer *English* Critick.

> (TE, VII, 18)

One must find 'the just Pitch of his Style', shunning both fustian and lowness. ''Tis a great Secret in Writing to know when to be plain, and when poetical and figurative.' In general Pope supports an intelligent fidelity to the Greek: 'I know no Liberties one ought to take, but those which are necessary for transfusing the Spirit of the Original, and supporting the Poetical Style of the Translation' (TE, VII, 17). Thus, although Pope's critics

said that one must not call the poem Homer, his own intention
was clearly to render the original accurately, if not slavishly.
He admired too a certain curtness in the older epics: '*Homer*
is in nothing more admirable than in the excellent Use he makes
of the *Silence* of the Persons he introduces', Pope remarks at
one point (*Il*, V, 848, note). His translation strives constantly
to balance the fullness and profusion of Homer's language –
what the Renaissance poet Sir John Davies called 'Homer's
abundant vein' – with this chastity and economy. Broadly
speaking, he was more successful in description than narration,
in discursive rather than episodic contexts: 'When he worked
with the couplet's natural bias for debate, assessment, organized
eloquence, and persuasion, as in the speeches, his achievement
was admirable.'[2] Even this can be accommodated within the
translator's view of his task, which was to get as near Homer
as the gap in time and cultural space permitted: 'He must be
content to imitate these Graces and Proprieties at more distance,
by endeavouring at something parallel, tho' not the same' (*Il*,
XIII, 720, note).

Technically this 'distance' was bridged by the evolution of a
unique poetic language. It drew on the accumulated 'epic' diction of Pope's predecessors – for example, Sylvester's translation of Du Bartas. It rested heavily on the example of Dryden's
Aeneid, and it occasionally enlisted Milton to perform the function of Homer's archaic and dialectical variations. To cite the
Preface again:

> Perhaps the Mixture of some *Graecisms* and old Words after
> the manner of *Milton* if done without too much Affectation,
> might not have an ill Effect in a Version of this particular
> Work, which most of any other seems to require a venerable
> *Antique* Cast.

> (TE, V, 19)

But as well as applying rust, Pope wanted to burnish English
idiom with energetic, forceful and impressive words. His choice
of diction was conditioned by the need to match Homer's conventional locutions and the formulaic devices of oral epic.
However, the Augustans usually found strength in limitation,
and Pope sought clarity and precision through his manipulation

of standard diction. We can see as much in this passage, translating a famous simile:

> But now, no longer deaf to Honour's Call,
> Forth issues *Paris* from the Palace Wall.
> In Brazen Arms that cast a gleamy Ray,
> Swift thro' the Town the Warrior bends his way.
> The wanton Courser thus, with Reins unbound,
> Breaks from his Stall, and beats the trembling Ground;
> Pamper'd and proud, he seeks the wonted Tides,
> And laves, in Height of Blood, his shining Sides;
> His Head now freed, he tosses to the Skies;
> His Mane dishevel'd o'er his Shoulders flies;
> He snuffs the Females in the distant Plain,
> And springs, exulting, to his Fields again.
> With equal triumph, sprightly, bold and gay,
> In Arms refulgent as the God of Day,
> The Son of *Priam,* glorying in his Might,
> Rush'd forth with *Hector* to the Fields of Fight.

> (*Il,* VI, 648-63)

The consciously pictorial effect is enhanced by the almost heraldic epithets (*brazen, shining, refulgent*). The 'Fields' at the end refer to the battle-ground, but also to the champaign country traversed by the 'courser' in the preceding comparison. The impression is left of heroic activity as the product of a fine instinct; the words catch the participants in full flight (note the repeated present participles). The horse's sweating flanks take on an intense gloss, just as Paris's armour throws off a dazzling gleam of light. In short, the grandeur and particularity of the scenic effects are used to create a spacious action and a note of high ceremony. Pope's diction enables us to look at events under the heroic aspect.

Similarly, in the *Odyssey,* when Telemachus assists Ulysses to kill the suitors, stylized language is employed to compose an almost ritual violence:

> With speed *Telemachus* obeys, and flies
> Where pil'd on heaps the royal armour lies;
> Four brazen helmets, eight refulgent spears,
> And four broad bucklers, to his Sire he bears:

At once in brazen Panoply they shone,
At once each servant brac'd his armour on;
Around their King a faithful guard they stand,
While yet each shaft flew deathful from his hand:
Chief after Chief expir'd at ev'ry wound,
And swell'd the bleeding mountain on the ground.
Soon as his store of flying fates was spent,
Against the wall he set the bow unbent:
And now his shoulders bear the massy shield,
And now his hands two beamy jav'lins wield;
He frowns beneath his nodding plume, that play'd
O'er the high crest, and cast a dreadful shade.

(*Od*, XXII, 126–41)

The menace of this scene owes much to a series of charged phrases like *bleeding mountain,* expressing at once physical distress and a kind of heroic elevation. John Arthos in his book on eighteenth-century diction quotes Milman Parry's description of the compound epithet in Homer as 'an incantation of the heroic', and rightly observes that stock locutions were used not just because of local contextual needs but also because of the charm felt to inhere in adopting 'the sanctified language of the fathers of poetry'.[3] (Brower similarly notes than the traditional epithet in Homer 'modifies not the immediate word or line...but the whole story, the whole heroic character'.)[4] Pope is trying to impart this same sense of familiarity – or, if you like, inevitability – to English words. Terms like 'flying fates' are used, not for surprise or 'poetic' effect, but in order to call up a host of memories and associations connected with arrows as the agents of destiny. The expression makes us think of arrows in one particular way – that is, as the accustomed mode of death in heroic contests, rather than as the sporting implements of merry men in Lincoln green.

As well as diction, there is Pope's incomparably resourceful versification. Maynard Mack has pointed out a number of variations which help to sustain rhythmic interest over the long haul of these two poems.[5] Perhaps the most notable of these devices is that of using a series of words (generally adjectives) with a strong trochaic accent – that is, a stressed syllable followed by

an unstressed. This falling rhythm cuts across the fundamental
rising pattern of iambic verse. A good example occurs as
Achilles is driving his way into Troy:

> And gasping, panting, fainting, labour on
> With heavier strides, that lengthen towards the Town.
>
> (*Il,* XXI, 636–7)

The movement of the first line suggests the jerky, uncoordinated
retreat of the Trojans to the safety of their city. Another example
cited by Mack comes as the funeral pyre is set up for Patroclus:

> First march the heavy Mules, securely slow,
> O'er Hills, o'er Dales, o'er Crags, o'er Rocks they go:
> Jumping high o'er the Shrubs of the rough Ground,
> Rattle the clatt'ring Cars, and the shockt Axles bound.
> But when arriv'd at *Ida's* spreading Woods,
> (Fair *Ida* , water'd with descending Floods)
> Loud sounds the Axe, redoubling Strokes on Strokes;
> On all sides round the Forest hurls her Oaks   147
> Headlong. Deep-echoing groan the Thickets brown;
> Then rustling, cracking, crashing, thunder down.
> The Wood the Grecians cleave, prepared to burn;
> And the slow Mules the same rough Road return.
>
> (*Il,* XXIII, 140–51)

Pope is obviously having fun playing phonetic games. The
enjambment of '*Headlong*' (147–8) reasserts with a thump the
event described; the cacophonous noises at the start are
matched by the endless drag of the long vowels in the final verse.
And once more we see that the trochaic accents of line 149
create a jolting, bumpy sound, precisely appropriate to the
sense. In fact, on a smaller scale, this rhythmic opposition
underlies much of the verse – to take two examples at random:

> Each warlike *Greek* the moving music hears,
> And iron-hearted Heroes melt in tears.
>
> (*Od,* XXIV, 79–80)

> They heard well pleas'd: the ready heralds bring
> The cleansing waters from the limpid spring:

> The goblet high with rosie wine they crown'd,
> In order circling to the peers around.
>
> (*Od,* XXI, 286–9)

In these cases stock diction combines with the falling accentual feet to lend a characteristic sound-pattern to the verse, one repeated hundreds of times throughout the two poems.

At the start of the *Odyssey,* Pope had contented himself with a 'General View' of epic, a reach-me-down compilation extracted from René le Bossu's treatise on the subject. It was the more natural, therefore, for him to add a Postscript to this later translation, especially as this gave him a chance to reply to Madame Dacier. In Pope's view the *Odyssey* 'is the reverse of the Iliad, in *Moral, Subject* and *Style*' (TE, X, 382). Nonetheless, he regards the two poems as equal in 'vivacity and fecundity of invention' and substantially equal in merit. Pope discusses the greater stylistic range of the *Odyssey,* and devotes some space to the prevailing Augustan dilemma of what to do about homely or 'low' language. He again mentions the practice of Milton's 'judiciously antiquated' style, comparing the admission of archaic words to 'the working old Abbey stones into a building' to give 'a venerable air' (390). However, the false sublime of Milton's imitators is rejected, and Pope states that his chief aim was 'to be easy and natural' in his rendering. Judged by modern standards, he has of course failed; but overall the *Odyssey* – collaborative and contrived as the enterprise was – stands up reasonably well to comparison with its predecessor. For Pope, Homer was a 'greater Genius' even than Virgil (TE, VII, 12) and 'the Father of Learning, a Soul capable of ranging over the whole Creation with an intellectual View, shining alone in an Age of Obscurity' (TE, VII, 80). He ended his account of Homer with the thought that writers might look on the poet's achievement 'with a Despair that it should ever be emulated with Success'. Luckily Pope himself was not cowed. Though his Homer project delayed him, it did not stunt his creative powers: indeed, he gained as a poet by this enterprise even more than he reaped as a shrewd professional. The Homer set him up imaginatively as well as financially.

*   *   *   *   *

Another venture of these years met with mixed results. When Pope lamented his condition in *The Dunciad*:

> Hibernian Politics, O Swift! thy fate;
> And Pope's, ten years to comment and translate.
>
> (*Dun*, B, III, 331–3)

he was joining with the Homer his editorial labours of the 1720s. These included an edition of the works of the Duke of Buckinghamshire, a high-toned nonentity of the usual Restoration model. Even this supererogatory act attracted attention in the panicky mood of the nation, and Pope's motives were scrutinized for Jacobite colouring. Much more important was the edition of Shakespeare which he undertook around 1721. The work took about three years. Again subscriptions were the main source of revenue when the six volumes appeared in 1725. A second edition came out in 1728, with some additional material from the Shakespearian apocrypha and elsewhere (like most editors until Malone in 1780, Pope omitted the Sonnets). Dr George Sewell, a hack with impeccable credentials for duncehood, was ironically chosen to oversee the additions. Pope had been given some help in collating the texts by Gay and his Homeric collaborator Elijah Fenton, but to tell the truth even this cooperative effort fell a long way short of what was needed.

The result was that Pope became involved in one of those dismaying contretemps which so often interrupted his career. He wrote in his Preface of having 'discharg'd the dull duty of an Editor, to [his] best judgment', and having exercised 'more labour' than he expected thanks.[6] This sounds unenthusiastic at best; and it is not surprising that a contemporary with more patience for the scholarly grind should have taken him up. This was Lewis Theobald, a creative writer by origin, who managed to live a double life as the deviser of foolish pantomimes and as a serious student of older (especially Elizabethan) literature. Theobald brought out in 1726 his detailed rebuke, *Shakespeare Restored: or, a Specimen of the Many Errors, as well Committed, as Unamended, by Mr. Pope in his late Edition of this Poet*. Although the title page went on to proclaim the author's true desire 'not only to correct the said Edition, but to restore the True Reading of Shakespeare in all the Editions ever yet publish'd', there can be no doubt that Theobald was gunning for Pope. And he hit the target, to the extent that a large number of detailed flaws were uncovered. Pope adopted a number of changes advocated by Theobald, though not very gracefully, in his second edition. But this was by no means the end of the story. Pope promptly enthroned Theobald as laureate of dullness in the original *Dunciad* (1728), whilst Theobald in turn brought out his own edition of Shakespeare in seven volumes (1733). Curiously, an assistant in this latter venture was William Warburton, later Pope's literary executor and most jealous defender on all aspects of doctrine and rectitude.[6]

Theobald has of late been more admired as a scholar than he was by his eighteenth-century successors, including Samuel Johnson. And the view was current for many years that Theobald had enjoyed a clear triumph over Pope. Perhaps we may be more cautious in awarding a unanimous verdict. It is certain that Theobald had read a great deal more Renaissance drama than Pope, and was much better versed in the 'background' to the subject. But he is prone to irrelevant analogues, often super-subtle, and seldom illuminating where dramatic issues are at stake, Pope, on the other hand, has the virtues of his defects. As *The Dunciad* makes plain, he had little patience with minute textual criticism, particularly when it was applied to vernacular works. The 'right verbal Critick', he explained, 'is to his Author as a Quack to his Patients, the more they suffer and complain the better he is pleas'd' (*Dun,* A, III, 188 note). Again, Pope accused Theobald, with some justice, of having 'laboured to prove *Shakespear* guilty of terrible *Anacronisms,* or low *Conundrums,* which Time had cover'd; and conversant in such authors as *Caxton* and *Wynkin,* rather than in *Homer* or *Chaucer'*(*Dun,* A, I, 164, note). Pope, of course, had a true Augustan scorn for 'Gothic' remnants. At the same juncture he quotes with approval a moderate poem called *On Verbal Criticism* (1733), written by a young Scot on the make called David Mallet. But Theobald managed to find an apt remark from Falstaff to put down Mallet (*2 Henry IV,* II, iv. 261) and the contest here was even.

The substantial area of Pope's superiority, however, lay not in scholarship but in taste. Although he took over from Nicholas

Rowe (a deceased friend, who had edited the plays in 1709) the biography which went, a little rejigged, into his first volume, the Preface itself was new and important. It has indeed some likeness to Samuel Johnson's great preface – one gets the same feeling of generosity struggling against hereditary blockages. Thus it is that the more famous remarks tend to seem patronizing today; as in the closing paragraph:

> I will conclude by saying of *Shakespear,* that with all his faults, and with all the irregularity of his *Drama,* one may look upon his works, in comparison with those that are more finish'd and regular, as upon an ancient majestick piece of *Gothick* Architecture, compar'd with a neat Modern building: The latter is more elegant and glaring, but the former is more strong and more solemn. It must be allow'd, that in one of these there are materials enough to make many of the other. It has much the greater variety, and much the nobler apartments; tho' we are often conducted to them by dark, odd, and uncouth passages. Nor does the Whole fail to strike us with greater reverence, tho' many of the Parts are childish, ill-plac'd, and unequal to its grandeur.

In some respects the tone here is misleading. Pope had after all characterized Shakespeare as 'the fairest and fullest subject for Criticism' among English poets. He 'would not omit any occasion' for praising Shakespeare. Again, 'he is not so much an Imitator, as an Instrument, of Nature'– an extraordinary admission at a time when the mimetic theory of art ruled everywhere. He is, in fact, the great 'original' – and this word is applied with every jot of the critical force it acquired later in the century, by which time Edward Young had invoked originality as the touchstone of great writing. Pope lays particular stress on the individuality of Shakespeare's characters: their refusal to merge, and their inward life. He speaks of the dramatist's hold on emotional experience (*'Power* over our *Passions'*), and wonders at the range of Shakespeare's portrayal of human character. Nor did Pope undervalue the ideas found in the plays, which he found all the more impressive because of Shake-

---

glaring striking, impressive

speare's supposed defects in education – 'He seems to have known the world by Intuition'. Of course, there are compensating flaws. But Pope is mainly concerned to exculpate Shakespeare on one ground or another. For his low fun the taste of the times is to blame – 'He writ to the People' – and his early lack of proper patronage excuses faults in what Pope took, rather shakily, to be the early works. Further, Shakespeare's own position in a company of actors limited his freedom as a creator. Pope is also inclined to think that partisan feeling on behalf of Ben Jonson had led to some deprecation of Shakespeare. In discussing this matter, Pope gets bogged down for a time in one of the dreariest arguments of the day – the question of Shakespeare's learning (or lack of it). The dispute runs through Dryden, Rowe, Dennis, Theobald, Johnson, Farmer and others.[7] Sometimes it is argued intelligently, sometimes foolishly, but almost always in profound ignorance. It is to Pope's credit that he devotes relatively little space to the topic. He emerges from the slough to such memorable statements as this: 'To judge therefore of *Shakespear* by *Aristotle's* rules, is like trying a man by the Laws of one Country, who acted under those of another.' And, equally noble in its way, 'From one or other of these considerations, I am verily perswaded, that the greatest and the grossest part of what are thought his errors would vanish, and leave his character in a light very different.' This is criticism at its warmest and most positive, as we find it throughout the Preface.

What of the edition itself? One feature which has caused comment is Pope's habit of signalling 'the most shining passages' by marginal marks, and sometimes awarding a star to an entire scene (occasionally there were marks of reprobation, indicating possible corruption). Officious as this may now strike us, it appears to have been received gratefully enough in its time: Warburton followed the same practice in his edition. And it does at least enable us to gauge Pope's taste with some precision, and to see just what it was in Shakespeare that vibrated in the Augustan soul. Slightly different views have been offered on this point; it is enough for the moment to say that Pope shows some independence in praising unpopular plays, but overall displayed the expected eighteenth-century preference for morally uplifting or philosophically powerful sections, rather than dramatically challenging junctures.[8] As for Pope's perfunctory verbal criticism, at least he provided one or two glosses which remain helpful. Shakespeare is still an obscure writer, and one would gladly trade in some of the hyper-elaborate scientific skills of modern bibliography for the rare ability in an editor to elucidate the darker meanings shortly and clearly.[9]

Pope often complained of the years he had spent on apparently non-creative tasks: 'I must again sincerely protest to you', he writes to a friend in 1722, 'that I have wholly given over scribbling, at least any thing of my own, but am become, by due gradation of dulness, from a poet a translator, and from a translator, a mere editor' (Corr, II, 140). But when he returned to 'scribbling' he found that the time had not been entirely wasted. His first major production after the break was the prose satire Peri Bathous, which draws heavily on his experience in the nooks and crannies of scholarship. The Dunciad made further levies upon this fund. And, as G. S. Rousseau has pointed out, Pope's 'editorial failure . . . taught him to limit the domain of his aesthetic ventures'.[10] We need not commiserate too deeply with him on account of his 'dull duty'; but like John Gay we may be ready to welcome Mr Pope back from his excursions.

CHAPTER SIX

❖

Maps of humanity

By the early 1730s Pope was back in full creative harness. So much so that he planned an ambitious scheme for a work in four parts, which proved indeed too ambitious ever to be realized. The poems we do have from this period are in many cases fragments of that unexecuted design. *An Essay on Man* was to be the opening book and so (as with Wordsworth's *Prelude*) we do have a central clue to the planned work. Later portions were to deal with such topics as government, education and morality. The four *Moral Essays* were originally intended to form part of this *magnum opus*; and it is likely that some of the political sections were incorporated into the *Imitations of Horace*. Pope speaks in a letter of drawing up 'a system of Ethics in the Horatian way' (*Corr*, iii, 81). From time to time he reports progress to his friends, identifying his purpose as that of putting morality in good humour. The 'Design' published with the *Essay* refers to 'some pieces of Human Life and Manners,' beginning with '*Man* in the abstract, his *Nature* and his *State*.' The present *Essay* is to be considered only as 'a *general Map* of MAN' (TE, III, i, 7–8).

It was certainly projected in 1730, if not earlier, but it was not published until 1733–4. Then the four epistles that make up the *Essay* were published at intervals over a period of eleven months. They appeared anonymously. On the surface, this was simply a ruse by which Pope could guarantee an impartial reception, and he did indeed succeed in drawing fulsome compliments from certain long-time antagonists. At a deeper level, perhaps, it was a way of announcing a new start – of marking a break with the earlier poems of satire and fantasy. It is a moot point whether Pope ever did transform the nature of his poetry, but he certainly liked to give the impression he had done so. Equally interesting is the division into four instalments. The *Moral Essays* were in the process of publication in exactly that form. Thomson's *Seasons* had come before the public in identical fashion a year or two earlier; and *Gulliver's Travels,* still less than a decade old, could easily have been issued with its four parts similarly separated. Moreover, Pope himself was soon to convert *The Dunciad* from its three-book to a four-book state, initially by the publication of a further instalment. Now it had been the habit of writers from antiquity onwards to invest their works with symbolic meanings relating to structure and numerology. But four had been only one magical number among many, and it is curious how the Augustans were drawn to this particular mode of symmetry – a shape soon to be reinforced by the evolution of the classical symphony. It is perhaps worth adding that other seminal books of the age appeared in four volumes (e.g. *Pamela*), though the form is less intrinsic here. It can hardly be doubted, however, that the tetrad appealed to Augustan notions of decorum more than the triad. There is something mystical, elusive, oblique about the latter, whereas a four-square pattern offers opportunities for echo, antithesis, balance. The plan of the intended work on ethics was evidently to constitute Pope's version of four quartets. Only the *Essay on Man,* the *Moral Essays* and *The Dunciad in Four Books* came to fruition.

In the first of these, Pope set out to reduce 'the science of Human Nature...to *a few clear points*'. We should be tempted to emphasize the verb. But contemporaries expected a writer to use his intelligence and learning to eliminate subtleties rather than to invent them. Pope considered it his duty to assimilate the canons of morality to bring them within the compass of ordinary sensible men and women. His intent is expository and not analytic. His style had to be perspicuous – but then it always was. His tone had to be approachable – public rather than introverted – and his argument immediately graspable. He wished to appear something very different from a harsh *raisonneur,* doling out crabbed philosophy to a sprinkling of academic specialists. He wished instead to convey the glitter and excitement of ideas to a broadly based lay public.

But nothing was further from his wishes than that he should find himself standing on a dais addressing empty space. The formal device employed, consequently, is that of four 'epistles' addressed to the statesman and philosopher (though some would dispute the titles) Viscount Bolingbroke. By this means Pope is able to adopt a casual, though not exactly intimate, manner. He can engage in asides, provoke objections, recapitulate and wander, in the certainty that his good-natured listener will sanction these things. The reader is flattered because the surrogate member of Pope's audience is such a distinguished personage. In fact, the reality is that personal correspondence, such as the term 'epistle' might indicate, is seldom in question. Bolingbroke's function is to mitigate the loneliness of the long-distance speaker, as when a nominal chairman is seated on the platform beside a public lecturer. He does not have to do anything. He just has to be there, to be complimented at start and end. Here (iv, 390) and elsewhere (IH, Ep. I, i, 177) Pope called Bolingbroke 'my Guide, Philosopher, and Friend' – the origin of this famous expression. In the *Essay* it is the last of these qualifications that explains Bolingbroke's presence.

It used to be thought that the philosopher was much in evidence, too. More than that – it was generally supposed that Bolingbroke had provided the matter for the *Essay* and Pope had simply versified what was given him. Nobody believes this any longer. On the other hand, the zeal with which Bolingbroke has been ushered off the poetic premises may have been over-officious. It is clear that Pope had his own views; clear that he was not indebted to Bolingbroke, Leibnitz or anyone else for the main drift of the argument; and clear that his poem is rooted in classical and Renaissance ethics. Nevertheless, this is not to say he was not influenced by later authorities. The survey of the origin of evil by William King (Archbishop of Dublin during Swift's time as Dean of St Patrick's) had been translated into English in 1731, and seems to underlie Pope's text more than once, e.g. at I, 241–2. And it is a guess rather than an established fact that Bolingbroke's philosophic remains postdate the *Essay*. All that can be safely said is that Pope *could* have written the poem without Bolingbroke's active participation. Whether or not he did is purely speculative.

The *Essay* soon provided controversy on an international scale. It was attacked by a Swiss protestant and, almost as bad, defended by a heavy footed English cleric on the make. This cleric later became a bishop, an assailant of Bolingbroke, and an editor of Shakespeare, as well as literary executor to Pope.

He did many valuable things; but William Warburton's defence
of the *Essay* as a model of irreproachable orthodoxy remains
hard to swallow. Voltaire admired the poem hugely as soon
as it came out, and showed its influence in a section on Pascal
he was adding to his *Lettres Philosophiques*. Other French admirers
included some of the later *philosophes*, for instance La Mettrie.
Pope had his French critics, too, notably among the Jansenists;
and perhaps his early translators ought to be listed among the
enemies of his reputation.[1]

Nowadays these doctrinal disputes do not ravage many
bosoms, and we respond to the *Essay* if at all as an imaginative
document. Sadly, even those who most delight in Pope find
it hard to get into the poem. This is not because of any special
failure on the author's part. It is rather because we have so little
practice in reading this kind of work. The modern world pro-
duces few theodicies, and virtually none of them in verse. Such
verse, too: alternately declamatory, lyrical, satiric, meditative –
seldom less than eloquent, unfailing in its resource and energy.
Yet we remain bemused, searching to find a legitimate occasion
for all this sumptuous writing. We pass from historical parallels
to character sketches and from natural description to moral
exhortation. The poetry is often (not quite always) impressive;
but we still miss the reason for its being.

A present-day reader, faced with these difficulties, will do
best to concentrate on the first epistle and the last. Between
them they contain most of the central doctrine and most of
the finest examples of Pope's art. Epistle I concerns 'the Nature
and State of Man, with respect to the Universe'. Its sets out
the view of creation as an ordered whole, made up of delicately
graduated scales of being from primitive life forms up to the
angels, with man in an intermediate position. The fourth part
is devoted to man 'with respect to Happiness'. It contains some
vivid sketches in Pope's sharpest satiric manner. In between
come an epistle on man in relation to himself as an individual
and another on man in relation to society. The former, leaving
aside its celebrated opening paragraph on 'the proper study
of Mankind', is lower in poetic pressure, whilst the latter is
generally conceded to be the weakest part of the *Essay*. It is
in the glowing metaphysical ardour of the first epistle, and the

keen sallies of the last, that the poem retains a kind of living even today.[2]

To be more specific: there is the urgent, exclamatory passage on infractions of Nature's order (I, 141–64), full of interjections, rhetorical questions and peremptory outbursts. There is the richly sensuous and evocative paragraph on the plenitude of Creation:

> Mark how it mounts, to Man's imperial race,
> From the green myriads in the peopled grass:
> What modes of sight betwixt each wide extreme,
> The mole's dim curtain, and the lynx's beam;
> Of smell, the headlong lioness between,
> And hound sagacious on the tainted green:
> Of hearing, from the life that fills the flood,
> To that which warbles thro' the vernal wood:
> The spider's touch, how exquisitely fine!
> Feels at each thread, and lives along the line...
>
> (I, 207–18)

Or the drunken cosmic dance (I, 251–6) reinvigorating the dead metaphors of scholastic thought. In the last epistle, we find colloquial ease (IV, 193–204), with a vivid comparison between cobbler and parson:

> One flaunts in rags, one flutters in brocade.

Pope develops his sceptical review of the bubble Fame, first taken up in his Chaucerian imitation almost twenty years before (IV, 237–58). Finally, a marvellous passage on the vanity of human wishes, moving from sharp mockery of contemporary nobodies dubbed Lord Umbra and Sir Billy to severe judgements on men like Bacon and Cromwell. The culmination is at once vehement and magnificently posed:

> If all, united, they ambition call,
> From ancient story learn to scorn them all.
> There, in the rich, the honour'd, fam'd and great,
> See the false scale of Happiness complete!
> In hearts of Kings, or arms of Queens who lay,
> How happy! those to ruin, these betray,

Mark by what wretched steps their glory grows,
From dirt and seaweed as proud Venice rose!
In each how guilt and greatness equal ran,
And all that rais'd the Hero, sunk the Man.
(IV, 285–94)

Sublime in their contempt, these lines were equalled only by
the portrait of Vice in the first *Epilogue to the Satires*. But even
such superb moments cannot wholly redeem the *Essay on Man*
for most readers. We admire the performance Pope puts on,
but we soon lose the thread. It is as though we were present
at some complicated lawsuit involving recondite points of
equity. We know the advocate is a good one; and yet we cannot
fathom his brief. The argument turns on too many forgotten
concepts, too many musty analogues. And we only ever consult
it in order to find out obsolete practice.

*   *   *   *   *

It comes as a surprise that the four *Moral Essays* belong to the
same scheme and indeed appear to have almost coalesced in
Pope's mind with the *Essay on Man*. They seem to us much better
examples of his mature skill. They give us not abstract specula-
tion (apart from the first half of the *Epistle to Cobham*) but lively
pictures of humanity in action. Pope has moved from dogma
and theory to the world of men and events, where he is always
at his strongest. According to the original plan, the *Essays* were
to form part of the last book concerned with '*Ethics,* or practical
Morality' – and it is worth stressing the adjective. The first two
epistles, as we now have them, were to comprise an introduction. We know, too, that Pope had intended to devote this
section on morality to the Cardinal Virtues, with two poems
considering the corresponding 'extremes' or vices (TE, III, ii,
XVIII–XXV). Again this is a strikingly Spenserian conception.
But the only remnant of this grand design is to be found in
the third and fourth epistles, which in the form they survive
incorporate the projected poems on avarice and prodigality.
We do not have anything corresponding to 'ye moderate use
of Riches', Pope's version of prudence. Nor do we know how
Pope would have approached the other virtues.

Actually *Moral Essays* is a misnomer; but it is not too damaging, and so long built into literary history that it is simpler to use the conventional title. Pope himself called them 'Epistles to Several Persons'. This draws attention to the recipient, as is right; each of the poems is governed in mood and treatment by the identity of the addressee. It also lays emphasis on the status of *epistles,* a term suggesting not any old letter (as one might write nowadays to one's bank manager) but a communication between friends – deliberated but informal, relaxed but not 'casual' in the offensive application. Pope jotted down many short memoranda to his business acquaintances, but he would not have termed these 'epistles', other than ironically. Correspondence included all sorts of missive, from the brief message we should now convey over the telephone to long formal compositions – dedications to the great, applications for grants or appointments, claims for redress, and so on. The familiar epistle was unlike either of these categories. It presupposed two people, near enough equal in standing to be able to mix socially, on paper as in life. They had, of course, to know each other reasonably well. They might have business to transact, which could be slipped into the letter; but the main burden of the correspondence must be more intimate: the exchange of news, or better still gossip; the expression of condolence or congratulation; the recollection of times past; the account of reflection or reading; the lament of the other's absence, or similar topics.

When the familiar epistle is shifted into poetry, an identifiable kind of rhetoric emerges. Pope always admired Horace, but it is in his verse epistles that the influence is most pervasive. He avoids the more declamatory effects of the *Essay on Man,* and seeks instead a comfortable, cheerful, companionable air. The best word for this approach is perhaps 'easy'. By this the Augustans did not mean total informality where anything goes. They thought rather of a serene and unintense outlook on life. The word is best defined by its opposites: the enemies of ease are affectation, pedantry, singularity, ceremoniousness and *hauteur.* It is, needless to say, a social concept. But it is equally a literary ideal, in so far as the values of the gentleman underwrote the artistic design of a genre like the epistle. To achieve ease was to establish rapport with one's audience; it derived from respect for others and for one's own medium.[3]

What does this involve, concretely, when we look at the text of these poems? It is registered first, in the language of the *Essays,* polished but not over-refined. The flow of the verse perfectly exemplifies the 'middle style' in poetry. It ranges from sharp colloquial touches (as in the racier parts of the *Epistle to Bathurst*) to the carefully mounted peroration which concludes the *Epistles to Burlington.* It involves ready use of vocative forms (as in the very first line addressed to Cobham), but equally a wide range of allusion. The writer can take on trust that his addressee will share a large fund of knowledge with him. Further, the structure of the epistle is conditioned by Pope's quest for an idiom of familiar ease. He can defend himself when required, answer objections, suggest qualifications. He can tell stories, point morals, draw characters, crack jokes. Some garrulity is forgivable, so long as the close tie between speaker and listener is not broken – if there is danger of this (as in *Bathurst,* line 338), the poet can exploit that very threat. Finally, the poet can use his friend as an object lesson. The argument can be clinched in the most economical (besides flattering) way, simply by appealing to the addressee's own qualities.

This is the pattern found in each of the epistles. It will be seen that the choice of a recipient is vital to the whole poetic effect. The poem now labelled Epistle I was in fact the third to be published, in 1734. It is addressed to Lord Cobham, a Whig grandee who had achieved some distinction as a soldier and was now cultivating more peaceful arts at Stowe, near Buckingham. Pope might possibly have been expected to resent Cobham's influence in Berkshire, where he had made himself the scourge of poachers and had helped to introduce a bevy of Hanoverian generals to take over the estates around Windsor. But Pope swallowed this, and his fiercely anti-Jacobite politics, for the sake of his devotion to matters of taste. These interests included the developing art of landscape gardening: Cobham employed men such as Bridgman, Kent and – after Pope's time – Capability Brown. This combined with a certain high-minded patriotism and classical aspirations to engender some fancifully named groves and arbours. Every summerhouse at

Stowe is a Temple of Liberty at the least; not an item of garden
furniture escapes its allotted literary or historical place. The
park was laid out, indeed, as a moral exhibition; to visit the
place was to take a mythological tour of man and society.[4] Pope
enjoyed all this – quite apart from getting his own bust set up
in a pantheon otherwise short of modern heroes, he responded
to the whole plan of constructing a *paysage moralisé* in the trim
Buckinghamshire countryside. It was everything he would have
liked to do, but could not, in his own little acre (five acres strictly)
at Twickenham, where everything had to be performed in
miniature.

Perhaps the poetic tribute to Cobham was meant to have
a connection with such landscapes of the mind. The last four
lines were certainly set on a memorial column at Stowe, many
years later; and it may be suggestive that Pope should have
explained that 'the first Epistle [was] to be to ye Whole work,
what a Scale is to a book of Maps'.[5] But the poem is too disjointed to supply any firm guidelines to Pope's system of ethics.
It starts brightly enough, but soon wanders off into abstract
generalities:

> Oft in the Passions' wild rotation tost,
> Our spring of action to ourselves is lost.
>
> (41–2)

It is not until we are deep into the epistle that this *Essay on
Man* vein is dispelled, and Pope launches into his most pointed
irony:

> A Saint in Crape is twice a Saint in Lawn;
> A Judge is just, a Chanc'lor juster still;
> A Gownman, learn'd; a Bishop, what you will;
> Wise, if a Minister; but, if a King,
> More wise, more learn'd, more just, more ev'rything.
>
> (88–92)

Then there is another lull before the poem picks up with some
graphic portraits culminating in Narcissa, immortalized within
six lines, and the miser Euclio, characterized entirely in a few
words of direct speech.

But the ending is abrupt and unsatisfactory. The trouble may have been that Pope simply did not know Cobham well enough – he strives to give the impression of cordiality, but one detects a slight constraint throughout. It is as though Pope had to be on his best behaviour. Hence the insistence on moral commonplace, driven home with explicit thoroughness, as on the theory of the Ruling Passions (166–79). Hence, too, the long delay in coming to the vital character sketches. And hence the stiffness of the argument, with its primly precise connectives: *Yet more; Not always Actions show the man; But grant that....; True; Know: Search then;* and so on. When Pope is in his happiest vein, he avoids these awkward devices, and shifts the point of the attack with far more adroit and inconspicuous 'ease'. The prominence of these connectives lends the discourse an air of well-meaning edification. Pope is drawing diagrams, as in the *Essay on Man,* and seems to be in need of a blackboard and some chalk. All this, as I say, seems to proceed from Cobham, with his dynastic pride and his noble patriot gestures. It is only intermittently that the epistle can escape striking comparable attitudes of its own. Then (as in the gross allusions of the last fifty lines) Pope shows what he could have done on such a topic. Overall, nonetheless, the 'Knowledge and Characters of Men' proves a disappointing theme, exposing Pope's weaknesses and offering few opportunities for his richest dramatizations of the human comedy.

Things are far better when we reach Epistle II, addressed 'To a Lady' and subtitled 'Of the Characters of Women'. The poem was the last to appear, a year after the one directed to Cobham. Its recipient was Martha Blount, a lifelong friend of Pope and a person whose tastes and sympathies he well understood. The tone is perceptibly more relaxed. In the opening lines Pope invites his listener to survey a portrait gallery of various women. She then remains a felt presence, though unmentioned, as we make our round of the gallery. At line 150, with the main series of characters completed, Pope turns to her again, inviting assent. The lady hesitantly offers a name in possible rebuttal of his case – which lends a special prominence to Pope's elaborate sketch of Cloe, which follows, and allows a smooth transition to his generalized reflections on the sex. After a passage of surpassing power on the fate of women, Pope turns back

to the lady, who has hitherto hovered on the edge of the poem,
and brings the work to a delicate conclusion with a warm recog-
nition of her particular virtues. The personal compliment serves
at the same time to dramatize ideal womanhood, and thus works
out the thematic design of the poem.

The earlier sections are extraordinary in their sparkle and
caustic description. We enter the poem as though catching Pope
and his friend in mid-exchange, debating a topic they have often
taken up in amicable discussion.

> Nothing so true as what you once let fall,
> 'Most Women have no Characters at all.'
>
> (1–2)

The expression 'let fall' immediately suggests unguarded confi-
dences, and the epistle continues in this intimate vein. There
is frequent recourse to a sort of cosy chattiness rare in Pope:

> Whether the Charmer sinner it, or saint it,
> If Folly grows romantic, I must paint it.
>
> (15–16)

The movement is free and colloquial:

> Sudden, she storms! she raves! You tip the wink,
> But spare your censure; Silia does not drink.
> All eyes may see from what the change arose,
> All eyes may see – a Pimple on her nose
>
> (33–6)

Elsewhere Pope indulges in direct mimicry of the fine lady's
accents:

> Papillia, wedded to her doating spark,
> Sighs for the shades – 'How charming is the Park!'
> A Park is purchas'd, but the Fair he sees
> All bath'd in tears – 'Oh odious, odious Trees!'
>
> (37–40)

Note the debased gallantry of *spark* and *fair,* and the petulant
repetition of *odious.* Yet with the trifling society chat there runs
a deeper strain, first hinted at when we come to the savage
contrast of

> ...Sappho at her toilet's greazy task,
> With Sappho fragrant at an evening Mask:
> So morning Insects that in muck begun,
> Shine, buzz, and fly-blow in the setting-sun.
>
> (25–8)

– a characteristic Popian conjunction of beauty and squalor.
The darker overtones become more pronounced with the
characters of Narcissa and Philomede, and burst into full
prominence with the cruel precision of the lines on Atossa:

> Full sixty years the World has been her Trade,
> The wisest Fool much Time has ever made.
> From loveless Youth to unrespected age,
> No Passion gratify'd except her Rage.
>
> (123–6)

The glories of the poem, however, reside principally in the
second half. First comes a moving evocation of the plight of
the female sex:

> See how the World its Veterans rewards!
> A Youth of frolicks, an old Age of Cards,
> Fair to no purpose, artful to no end,
> Young without Lovers, old without a Friend,   246
> A Fop their passion, but their Prize a Sot,   247
> Alive, ridiculous, and dead, forgot!
>
> (243–8)

Pope's supreme technical mastery was never used to better purpose. Notice, for example, how the switch from plural to singular in line 246 encapsulates the situation: a woman might like
many lovers in her youth, but a single friend would satisfy her
in lonely old age. Observe too the marvellous phonetic architecture of line 247, where the chiming monosyllables *fop* and
sot assert their identity across the full space of the metre – the
medial conjunction *but* is thus turned towards the sense 'and
so (of course)'. It is a beautiful demonstration of the flexibility
of antithesis, so often written off as a monotonous and limited
device.

This high point could not be sustained for long. But with

consummate skill Pope drops his voice, addresses his friend
directly, and celebrates her good humour in the minor trials
of life:

> Oh! – blest with Temper, whose unclouded ray
> Can make to morrow chearful as to day;
> She, who can love a Sister's charms, or hear
> Sighs for a Daughter with unwounded ear;
> She, who ne'er answers till a Husband cools,
> Or, if she rules him, never shows she rules;
> Charms by accepting, by submitting sways,
> Yet has her humour most, when she obeys;
> Let Fops or Fortune fly which way they will;
> Disdains all loss of Tickets, or Codille;
> Spleen, Vapours, or Small-pox, above them all,
> And Mistress of herself, tho' China fall.
>
> (257–68)

The lines are irradiated by that very cheerful lack of fuss which
Pope is describing. Then the beautifully turned tribute:

> Be this a Woman's Fame: with this unblest,
> Toasts live a scorn, and Queens may die a jest.
> This Phoebus promis'd (I forget the year)
> When those blue eyes first open'd on the sphere;
> Ascendant Phoebus watch'd that hour with care,
> Averted half your Parents simple Pray'r,
> And gave you Beauty, but deny'd the Pelf
> That buys your sex a Tyrant o'er itself.
> The gen'rous God, who Wit and Gold refines,
> And ripens Spirits as he ripens Mines,
> Kept Dross for Duchesses, the world shall know it,
> To you gave Sense, Good-Humour, and a Poet.
>
> (281–92)

It is as though the empty gallantries of Restoration verse have
been endowed with a social conscience. This makes for praise
as judicious in its bestowal as agreeable in its surface politeness.

The so-called 'third' of the *Epistles* was originally published in

---

Codille   In the card-game 'Ombre', as played in *ROL*.

1733. It is addressed to a rakish Tory gentleman, Allen Bathurst, who had been promoted to a barony in 1711 as part of a political manoeuvre to ensure the passage of the Peace of Utrecht. The theme this time is identified by a subtitle, 'Of the Use of Riches', and indeed money is the overriding concern. In eighteenth-century terms Bathurst was himself an 'easy' kind of man, debonair, unruffled, unconstrained. Pope had built up a splendidly open friendship with him – their letters are full of mock reproach, which is the sure sign of an Augustan intimacy. On the other hand, it was a more robust relationship, naturally enough, than that of Pope with Martha Blount. The note is masculine, the humour often bawdy, the overall impression a little cynical and worldly. Pope brings these lineaments of his friend's personality into the very fabric of the discourse – and that is the essential trick of these familiar epistles.

Nowadays the poem tends to be read rather solemnly. True, there are a number of Biblical overtones, as in the 'parable' of Sir Balaam. True also that Pope confronts a number of important economic issues of the time.[6] And true, finally, that he lavished a good deal of care on the poem – it was 'as much laboured as any one of my works'. In particular, he strove hard to make his portrait of the charitable Man of Ross (249–90) a symbolic restatement of the theme of benevolence. But the better parts of the epistle are not the careful lapidary lines devoted to this charitable paragon, but the swingeing attacks on venal politicians, the sudden lunges against grasping financiers, the comic hyperbole and fantastic invention:

> Blest paper-credit! last and best supply!
> That lends Corruption lighter wings to fly!
> Gold imp'd by thee, can compass hardest things,
> Can pocket States, can fetch or carry Kings;
> A single leaf shall waft an Army o'er,
> Or ship off Senates to a distant Shore;
> A leaf, like Sybil's, scatter to and fro
> Our fates and fortunes, as the winds shall blow:
> Pregnant with thousands flits the Scrap unseen,
> And silent sells a King or buys a Queen.
>
> (69–78)

Here is 'audacious contemporaneity' indeed! And yet there is also something modern about this vision of financial skulduggery, realized with brilliant economy in a succession of curt, dismissive verbs – *imp'd, compass, pocket, fetch and carry, waft, ship off, scatter, flits, sells*. There is a submerged metaphor here, connected with the cargo trade. Pope makes public credit into a kind of dishonest broker, dealing in nations as others deal in tea or calicoes.

Another way of indicating the particular power of the poem would be to say that (for the first time, almost) the topical significance outweighs the moral suggestiveness of the declared theme. We may not be persuaded in every detail as regards the critique of riches; the picture of avarice in action (old Cotta) is not entirely convincing as a Theophrastian setpiece. But it is superb as dramatized biography. Similarly with Sir Balaam at the end. Whatever the merit of the parable, there is no question of the narrative qualities of this episode. Pope rushes us headlong through a crowded life history, his syntax elliptical and his vocabulary close to every vulgar detail of actuality:

> The Tempter saw his time; the work he ply'd;
> Stocks and Subscriptions pour of ev'ry side,
> 'Till all the Daemon makes his full descent,
> In one abundant show'r of Cent. per Cent.,
> Sinks deep within him, and possesses whole,
> Then dubs Director, and secures his soul.
>   Behold Sir Balaam, now a man of spirit,
> Ascribes his gettings to his parts and merit,
> What late he call'd a Blessing, now was Wit,
> And God's good Providence, a lucky Hit.
> Things change their titles, as our manners turn;
> His Compting-house employ'd the Sunday morn:
> Seldom at Church ('twas such a busy life)
> But duly sent his family and wife.
> There (so the Dev'l ordain'd) one Christmas-tide
> My good old Lady catch'd a cold, and dy'd.....
>
> (369–84)

And then, after Sir Balaam's second marriage to a fashionable lady:

> My Lady falls to play; so bad her chance,
> He must repair it; takes a bribe from France;
> The House impeach him; Coningsby harangues;
> The Court forsake him, and Sir Balaam hangs;
> Wife, Son and daughter, Satan, are thy own,
> His wealth, yet dearer, forfeit to the Crown;
> The Devil and the King divide the prize,
> And sad Sir Balaam curses God and dies.
>
> (395–402)

In one way this is as close as Pope ever gets to the novel; in another, as close as he gets to light verse, as W. H. Auden understood that. Throughout the hectic rush of events, Pope never loses control of our responses. Even in the haste, every word counts (*dubs*; *turn*; *dearer*; *sad*). One notices how 'harangues', which always seems to need a predicate, is left stranded here, leaving the impression of a routine oration to which nobody listens. The language reflects in itself the commercial debasement of spiritual matters (*a lucky Hit*; *show'r*, stripped of its Biblical associations). Pope manages to express a whole social philosophy in this rapid narrative. He exposes the City life style as in *The Dunciad* he portrayed the City culture, and he borrows the City slang to do it.

Placed last in the collected *Epistles*, but the first to be written, the poem addressed to the Earl of Burlington has been among the most admired works in the canon of late. Originally subtitled 'Of False Taste', the formula 'Of the Use of Riches' was later applied here too. But now we are viewing the topic aesthetically rather than economically. Again this is appropriate: for where Bathurst was a slightly coarse-grained politician, Burlington was a man of taste to his fingertips. He was an architect of some distinction, a patron and a connoisseur. The poem, indeed, was stated on its first appearance in 1731 to have been 'Occasion'd by [Burlington's] Publishing Palladio's Designs of the Baths, Arches, Theatres, &c. of Ancient Rome' – something his lordship never got around actually to completing. The relationship between Pope and Burlington was more distant than the Pope–Bathurst friendship: there was more respect and admiration in it, less genuine human warmth. So Pope was enabled to call on his grandest manner. The poetry bristles with its own nobility. High sententious phrasing, orotund Roman diction, dignified port are all much in evidence. Witness the conclusion:

> You too proceed! make falling Arts your care,
> Erect new wonders, and the old repair,
> Jones and Palladio to themselves restore,
> And be whate'er Vitruvius was before:
> Till Kings call forth th'Idea's of your mind,
> Proud to accomplish what such hands design'd,
> Bid Harbors open, public Ways extend,
> Bid Temples, worthier of the God, ascend;
> Bid the broad Arch the dang'rous Flood contain,
> The Mole projected break the roaring Main;
> Back to his bounds their subject Seas command,
> And roll obedient Rivers thro' the Land;
> These Honours, Peace to happy Britain brings,
> These are Imperial Works, and worthy Kings.
>
> (191–204)

Burlington must have been delighted with this. It is exactly calculated to flatter his own aspirations for himself. He had that scholarly conservatism which would rather be Palladio restored than Vanbrugh (let us say) original. And he functioned as a kind of Minister of Culture, directing and designing while others executed. Moreover, the sweep of the verse pays homage to his selfconscious munificence. You cannot write tributes like this in the poetic manner of Verlaine or Philip Larkin.

Luckily the epistle is not limited to such declamatory effects. Much of it is superb comedy, delineating the world of a very different great man – Timon, whom contemporaries (perhaps wrongly) insisted on identifying with the Duke of Chandos.[7] It is arguable that Timon outgrows his place in the structure, as an anti-type of the theme – examplar, that is, of false taste or the misuse of riches. But one must be chary of talking too schematically about the 'structure' of an epistle. What Pope gives us is not a systematic discourse. It is rather a dynamic, living

argument, in which metaphors, anecdotes, allegories and satiric
cameos are dramatically thrust up against one another. Timon
elicits such gorgeously funny writing that other considerations
are swept aside – the poem can afford to wait while we make
a prolonged tour of his estate; Pope's carriage is at the door,
and will carry us away at the right time.

In all literature there are few more devastating portraits of
vulgar ostentation. Timon does not even have the excuse of
being a *nouveau riche*: he is a (very) full-blown aristocrat. Again
and again the language punctures his pretensions: his music
is all *quirks* (142), his painted saints *sprawl* on the ceiling (146),
his tritons *spew* (154), his buildings are mere *heaps* (109), his
ornamental Cupids *squirt* (111) – and so on. The attack is
mounted with the full panoply of traditional rhetoric. Pope
several times employs paradox in its strictest form, oxymoron:

> Trees cut to Statues, Statues thick as trees,
> With here a Fountain, never to be play'd,
> And there a summer-house, that knows no shade...
>
> (120–2)

Similarly seagods wither in dry alcoves; finely bound books
gather dust unread in a show library; the chapel provides 'all
the Pride of Prayer' (142); and finally at the dinner table:

> In plenty starving, tantaliz'd in state,
> And Complaisantly help'd to all I hate,
> Treated, caress'd, and tir'd, I take my leave,
> Sick of his civil Pride from Morn to Eve;
> I curse such lavish cost, and little skill,
> And swear no Day was ever past so ill.
>
> (163–8)

Everything is perverted from its natural function. And everything is out of proportion – hence the second major recourse,
hyperbole. As Pope tells us at the outset,

> Greatness with Timon, dwells in such a draught
> As brings all Brobdignag before your thought.
>
> (104–5)

There is an irony here, in that the 'Brobdignag' of *Gulliver's Travels*
was ruled by a beneficent lord – a very Burlington, perhaps

we are meant to reflect. Against this, Timon's villa stands, vain, ugly and monstrous. Its size is the measure of its owner's little-ness – a truly Augustan inversion of scale.

Yet after this exuberant setpiece, the poem instantly retracts to a moral commonplace (169–72), and then steps forward again with renewed confidence. It is one of the most splendid moments in all Pope – the cumulated energies of the poem are invested in two exquisite quatrains. One is elegiac and contemplative; the other, outgoing and prophetic:

> Another Age shall see the golden Ear
> Imbrown the Slope, and nod on the Parterre,
> Deep Harvests bury all his pride has plann'd,
> And laughing Ceres re-assume the land.
>   Who then shall grace, or who improve the Soil?
> Who plants like BATHURST, or who builds like BOYLE.
> 'Tis Use alone that sanctifies Expence,
> And Splendour borrows all her rays from Sense.
>
> (173–80)

The second quatrain might have been a mere inert 'commer-cial'; but the design of the poem is such that Pope's compliment sits happily alongside the evocative lines that precede it. Such is the capacity of the familiar epistle, in the hands of a master.

Boyle   i.e. Burlington (the family name)

CHAPTER SEVEN

Images of life

No department of Pope's writing enjoys readier appreciation today than his *Imitations of Horace*. He embarked on these free adaptations of epistles and satires by the Roman poet early in 1733. As well as the main series of poems he produced two modernized versions of Donne and one or two allied works. The *Epistle to Dr Arbuthnot* (1735) was later designated by Warburton 'the Prologue to the Satires'. This was probably without Pope's authority, but it is a perfectly apt title all the same. Two separate dialogues, on the other hand, were written in 1738 and expressly labelled by Pope two years later 'Epilogue to the Satires'. A fragment called *Seventeen Hundred and Forty,* first published in 1797, is generally regarded as a pendant to this series.

The imitation of an older (normally classical) poem was a favourite Augustan mode. It permitted the kind of dramatic interplay between ideas and attitudes in which contemporaries so often delighted. It is not a strict translation, though it rarely strays far from the literal sense of the original. Rather than paraphrasing his model, the poet seeks to bring out its relevance in the immediate historical situation. The argument of the ancient writer is preserved; the aim is to slip in modern instances. Pope was proud of the fidelity with which he followed Horace, to the extent of printing a parallel Latin text alongside his own lines. He chose as his basic 'copy text' a conservative edition of Horace put out by Daniel Heinsius about a century before. But he seems to have admitted a number of readings which had quite lately been proposed by Richard Bentley, the tempestuous scholar at the centre of many an eighteenth-century *Kulturkampf*. The reasons for printing the Latin were varied. It made comparison possible, and thus drew attention to Pope's ingenuity (and occasionally scholarship). It accounted for certain episodes or references which might otherwise have seemed awkward. And it excused certain improprieties. Finally, it provided at once a touchstone and a seal of quality. It was a way of establishing his credentials to do for the England of George

Augustus what Horace had done for the Rome of Octavian, later Augustus Caesar. Horace's text in a manner of speaking endorses the product.

Throughout the Restoration and eighteenth century, Horace was among the most congenial of poets to an English audience. His *Art of Poetry,* or epistle to the Pisones (a father and two sons), was translated, reprinted, imitated, burlesqued. His odes retained a secure hold on public affection, and a commendation made in 1652, 'Horace, the best of lyrick Poets', would have found a ready assent for a century of more. There was a steady flow of English renderings of the complete works and of selected items: the version of *Odes, Satyrs and Epistles* by Thomas Creech (1681) was standard for several generations, though Philip Francis's translation began to rival it from the 1740s. The currency of the *Satires* and *Epistles* was perhaps marginally greater, but educated people would at least pretend to some acquaintance with the canon virtually in its entirety.

The first book of *Satires* contains ten poems in hexameters. It probably dates from about 35 B.C. and constitutes Horace's first collection. The second book, with eight satires, followed some five years later. The next period was given over to lyric verse, with the *Epodes* and earlier *Odes* making their appearance. The twenty epistles which make up the first book were published around 20 B.C. in all probability. The short second book, with the *Epistle to Augustus* set at its head, came out not long before Horace's death in 8 B.C. To this last period belong the last book of the *Odes,* the *Carmen Seculare* and the *Art of Poetry,* which is improperly joined to the *Epistles* by later scholiasts.

Satire was already a considerable form in Rome, though Horace is the first of the really great practitioners. On the other hand we have to delve in some obscure corners to find much of a lineage for the verse letter: there was no live tradition to aid the writer here. In both forms Horace achieved a friendly, urbane tone, one which could achieve dignity without undue weight, seriousness without solemnity, urgency without shrillness. The eighteenth century particularly admired in Horace his capacity for 'raillery', a fine wit applied to constructive rather than destructive ends. This goes with a degree of oblique irony and a gentle amusement. The ideal is a searching yet tolerant gaze on men and affairs: the satirist must not appear to be fanatical, loud or malicious. In fact this is a standard which Horace does not always meet, and which often gets completely forgotten in the growing vehemence of Pope's imitations, especially where politics rears its head. Nevertheless the image of Horace was of a *smiling* public man, discoursing equably to an intelligent audience (witness his own term for the satires, *sermones,* or causeries). He was seen as an intensely moral poet, but neither stern nor hectoring. To the extent that Pope departs from his model of affable honesty, he could rely on contemporary readers to deduce that this was a conscious departure, and that it indicated something about modern England as a vehicle of satire.[1]

Nevertheless, it is a fact (regrettable as it may be) that the *Imitations* must stand on their own feet today. They can derive little support from Horace; even if his text is printed, only a minority of readers will be sufficiently at home with the nuances of the Latin to pick up every shade of meaning, tone or allusion. What we tend most to enjoy about the poems, to be honest, is in part an unHoratian quality. That is, a nervous excitement, generated by a succession of moods – aggressive, defensive; cheerful, embittered; good-humoured, angry; and many other emotional states glancing over the surface of the poem. We respond to the vigorous freedom of the language, and the chameleon-like poses of the satirist. Pope constantly dramatizes his own condition, sometimes ruefully deploring his harsh fate in life, at other times musing autobiographically on the years gone by. The rhythm is impulsive; often conversation is introduced directly into the poem, with a metrical skill born of Pope's long apprenticeship. Paradoxically, it is just because he had laboured so hard to achieve the finest polish that he could make his verse so freely colloquial and yet avoid the 'roughness' of earlier English satirists. He enlisted all his experience to produce an effect of negligent ease:

> My lands are sold, my Father's house is gone,
> I'll hire another's, is not that my own,
> And yours my friends? thro' whose free-opening gate
> None comes too early, none departs too late;   158

> (For I, who hold sage Homer's rule the best,
> Welcome the coming, speed the going guest.)
> 'Pray heav'n it last! (cries Swift) as you go on;
> I wish to God this house had been your own:
> Pity! to build, without a son or wife:
> Why, you'll enjoy it only all your life.' –
> Well, if the Use be mine, can it concern one
> Whether the Name belong to *Pope* or *Vernon?*
> What's *Property?* dear Swift! you see it alter
> From you to me, from me to Peter Walter,   168
> Or, in a mortgage, prove a Lawyer's share,
> Or, in a jointure, vanish from the Heir,
> Or in pure Equity (the Case not clear)
> The Chanc'ry takes your rents for twenty year:
> At best, it falls to some ungracious Son
> Who cries, my father's damn'd, and all's my own.
>
>   (Sat. II, ii, 155–74)

The idiom here is familiar but not indecorous. Notice how in line 158 the homely expression yet makes a perfect antithesis; and how in line 168 there is the same effect of conversational spontaneity achieved through standard rhetorical means. The name-dropping intimacy of the discourse is pointed up by the rhymes, which seem almost to have fallen from heaven – 'from me to – well, anyone you care to name, even Peter Walter' (he was an infamous financial wheeler-dealer). 'Vernon' was Pope's own landlord.

The *Epistle to Arbuthnot,* though it takes no direct hint from Horace, is altogether of a piece with the imitations proper. It recalls the third satire of the second book, actually, in its constant allusion to madness:

> The Dog-star rages! nay 'tis past a doubt,
> All *Bedlam,* or *Parnassus,* is let out:
> Fire in each eye, and Papers in each hand,
> They rave, recite, and madden round the land.   (3–6)

The tone is mock exasperated; for much of the poem, we feel a medley of confused emotions. The world seems lunatic, i.e. disordered *but comic.* The *Epistle* can be read as a drama of mixed

feelings, in which Pope confronts his own identity as an artist.
There is a good deal of autobiography, as is natural in a communication addressed to a friend of such long standing (Pope
throughout trades on this relationship, confident that his friend
will decode without trouble every private joke and public allusion). But the poem is more than a personal apologia. The
theme is 'Wit, and Poetry, and *Pope*' (26). This indicates not
revelation of the poet's soul, as it might be for a Romantic;
rather an assertion of the social function of the writer. In the
course of the *Epistle* Pope claims a right to well-earned privacy;
but at the same time he displays a sharp awareness of the need
for satire to go out into the world. A pastoralist may retreat
to the green shades of Windsor. But Pope is halfway towards
the city, where he knows he can reach people and be reached
('All fly to *Twit'nam*,' 21). This makes an apt introduction to
the main series of imitations. In them, as nowhere else to the
same degree, Pope makes his way into the everyday world –
what Maynard Mack calls 'the long diurnal haul'. This is the
familiar environment of our ordinary existence, 'in its noonday
hubbub, its humdrum practicality, its muted passions that
nevertheless gleam like diamonds in the compression of a
phrase: in its crowds and chandeliers and coffee-spoons...'.[2]

The poem was put together over a number of years and incorporates several earlier fragments. Yet it never reads like a cento
of disconnected passages. When it was assembled, in 1733 or
1734, Pope managed to give his verse letter a strong impetus
of its own. He moves from indulgent laughter to dignified self-
defence; he inserts fierce attacks on individuals (Addison, 193–
214; Lord Hervey, 305–33). But these are no deflections from
his central task; the loathsome insect 'Sporus' is included
because the poem dictates it, not just because Pope's emotions
require it:

> Whether in florid Impotence he speaks,
> And, as the Prompter breathes the Puppet squeaks;
> Or at the Ear of *Eve,* familiar Toad,
> Half froth, half Venom, spits himself abroad,
> In Puns, or Politicks, or Tales, or Lyes,
> Or Spite, or Smut, or Rymes, or Blasphemies.

> His Wit all see-saw between *that* and *this,*
> Now high, now low, now Master up, now Miss,   324
> And he himself one vile Antithesis.
> Amphibious Thing! that acting either Part,
> The trifling Head, or the corrupted Heart!
> Fop at the Toilet, Flatt'rer at the Board,
> Now trips a Lady, and now struts a Lord.
>
>   (317–29)

This is a wickedly composed allegory of evil, personified in the androgynous courtier Hervey. The iconography, so to speak, is all to do with sexual perversion – impotence, bisexual tastes, squeaky voice, smutty talk. His very foppishness compounds the dirt which hangs about his person. As a recent critic puts it, 'with great psychological acuteness Pope represents the chaos of personal energies which is the psyche of Sporus.... Somehow Pope intuited from Hervey's drawing room manner substantially everything which we can . . . couch in psychological terms. He expressed what he perceived in the language available to him and hence portrayed Sporus/Hervey as Evil incarnate.'[3] And this chaos is rendered with merciless precision in the seesaw of lines 324–5, the over-finicky antitheses, and the easy alternation of roles mirrored in the final couplet. Hervey's 'Politicks', we deduce, are a dirty hole-and-corner business like his bawdy chatter. He jumps when the prompter (Walpole, no doubt) says 'jump'; he intrigues with Eve (Queen Caroline) – again there is a suggestion of lubricity, though Sporus can produce only froth and venom, not semen. It is a horrific picture, and more rather than less so because of the refinement of Pope's technique.

Yet this is not the last word. As so often, Pope ends in a more positive key. Here he celebrates a good man in the person of his own father, and asks heaven to preserve his friend. This was a forlorn hope, as Pope knew; Dr Arbuthnot was dying, and in fact survived publication of the poem (on 2 January 1735) by a bare seven weeks. Mortality had thrust itself into the *Epistle* at various points ('this long Disease, my Life', 132); and Arbuthnot had been thanked for preserving Pope's own fragile existence. Yet the conclusion is more than a pious gesture of gratitude. It celebrates friendship and the 'social, chearful, and serene' life Arbuthnot had led (416). These epithets represent the ideal from which Pope felt himself debarred by his personal history and his artistic vocation. The ultimate drift of the *Epistle* is to laud domestic virtue, whilst showing it as always unattainable to the embattled satirist.[4]

Pope wrote six full-scale imitations of Horace, disregarding a portion of another (Sat. II, vi) substantially by Swift, and one which he attempted 'in the manner of Dr. Swift' (Ep. I, vii). There is also *Sober Advice from Horace* (1734), which stands a little apart. It is a version of Sat. I, ii, in which Horace writes on the theme of sexuality with a freedom that Pope found quite infectious. It was excluded from Pope's own collections for some time, and after his death Warburton removed it once more. Whatever we think of this officious act, it is apparent that the poem takes its erotic function too seriously to make any great artistic claim. Every opportunity for innuendo is taken:

> When sharp with Hunger, scorn you to be fed,
> Except on *Pea-Chicks,* at the *Bedford-head?*
> Or, when a tight, neat Girl, will serve the Turn,
> In errant Pride continue stiff, and burn?
>
> (149–52)

This is just what Horace says, leaving aside the Bedford Head and with the omission of a handy serving boy. But there is a limit to the literary interest of such sly rescensions, and Pope reaches it pretty soon.

We are left, then, with two satires (both from the second book), and two epistles from each book. It is best to take them in this order. They were published at intervals between 1733 and 1738. The order of composition is not important. Each is addressed to an identifiable individual; all were friends of Pope (except in the case of the insolent dedication 'To Augustus'), some being prominent men, others relatively obscure. Generally Pope finds a direct equivalent for the Horatian addressee, but he is more concerned to find an appropriate recipient for his *own* purposes – that is, someone whose presence will colour the discourse in the desired manner.

A good example is the first imitation to appear, Sat. II, i.
All round this is one of the most successful attempts to find
'an Answer from Horace', as the advertisement at its head puts
it. That has something to do with the figure Pope chose to replace
Trebatius – William Fortescue, a distinguished advocate who in
time became a judge and then Master of the Rolls. Fortescue
had subscribed to the *Iliad* and by the early 1720s had made
the acquaintance of Pope. He advised the poet on financial
and legal matters, notably the protection of his copyright
against Curll *et hoc genus omne*. Fortescue was often out on the
circuit, so the two men corresponded freely over twenty years
and more. This fact is crucial to the imitation. Pope starts off
like a humble litigant briefing his barrister:

> Tim'rous by Nature, of the Rich in awe,
> I come to Council learned in the Law.   (7–8)

But it soon emerges there is to be no fee (as usual, we understand); and Pope quickly establishes a bantering, undeferential
tone. This is vital, because the poem proceeds through rapid
exchanges – and we have to feel that the two speakers are equal.
Of course, Fortescue is presented as sage and worldly; he
cautions Pope against offending the mighty. He is given a bar-
barous legal jargon to mouth – precedents, maxims, statutes.
And he is forced to expose himself more fully than had Trebatius.
Horace uses the lawyer as a straight man, offering up easy lobs
for the satirist to kill. Trebatius holds the majesty of the law
in high respect, but he seems to have some genuine concern
lest his friend should get into trouble. Fortescue, on the other
hand, is made to embody the worst aspects of a professional
'expert' – he recommends timeserving and deceit. His very
speech is prevaricating, anodyne, pedantic, as experts are often
held to be:

> Your plea is good. But still I say, beware!
> Laws are explain'd by Men – so have a care.
> It stands on record that in *Richard*'s Times
> A Man was hang'd for very honest Rhymes.
> Consult the Statute: *quart*. I think it is,
> *Edwardi Sext*. or *prim. & quint. Eliz*:
> See *Libels, Satires* – here you have it – read.   (143–8)

Pope pretends to comply. Characteristically, the lawyer is satisfied when the poet announces that he will write 'grave *Epistles*' to ingratiate the Court. As the poem makes clear, he was in fact redoubling the force of his satire, working all the time towards greater specificity and point.

The whole epistle shows the writer as inalienably in conflict with the legal machinery and indeed the administrative hocus pocus of a modern state. It is not surprising that Pope felt it necessary (unconvincingly) to assure Fortescue he was not the friend written into the poem. He probably had no wish to offer Fortescue personally any insult; but he did intend to show lawyers as handmaidens of the new governmental apparatus. What that meant for satire, the poem expresses. *Virtue,* for the first time, is used in explicitly political terms:

> Can there be wanting to defend Her Cause,
> Lights of the Church, or Guardians of the Laws?
>
> (109–10)

What could be a self-gratulatory pose ('The Feast of Reason and the Flow of Soul' attend Pope and his out-of-place friends in their 'retreat') is redeemed by our awareness that Pope is addressing one who helps to keep the Establishment intact. Pope is steadily politicizing Horace. The Latin poem, one might say, is about defamation as a civil crime: the English poem is about official secrets.

Very different is the second satire of the second book. As Pope (following Horace) says at the start, its 'doctrine' is none of his. At least, it is put into the mouth of another. Horace had his tribute of the simple life expressed by Ofellus, described as a poor tenant farmer working hard to restore his finances after having been dispossessed. Pope, on the other hand, chooses Hugh Bethel, a country squire rather than a yeoman farmer; and one with strong metropolitan links. Instead of deploring the loss of Ofellus's land, Pope ends by dilating upon the fragility of property in general terms. Since Bethel was well off, it would have been absurd, as well as ungracious, to follow the original at this point. Moreover, where Horace seems to be reporting the views of Ofellus throughout, Pope takes over in his own voice in the middle of the poem. The effect is to dramatize a colloquy, rather than simply recount opinions. And again there is a sense of equality; Bethel is mildly rallied at the start ('Sermon' seems an ominous translation of *Sermo*), but he soon reveals a capacity to tell a tale. And he commands a colloquial vigour we all might envy:

> *Oldfield*, with more than Harpy throat endu'd,
> Cries, 'Send me, Gods! a whole Hog *barbecu'd*!'
> Oh blast it, South-winds! till a stench exhale,
> Rank as the ripeness of a Rabbit's tail.
> By what *Criterion* do ye eat, d'ye think,
> If this is priz'd for *sweetness,* that for *stink*?
>
> (25–30)

The language is homely, even gross in its concrete particularity. Food is everywhere – not merely choice cooked dishes but also the raw article. And Pope confronts the nature of true hospitality, contrasting it with the cloying richness of a City feast. Bethel, then, stands for moderation, good sense, and 'natural' pleasures of the body, as against rampant sensuality. He is not just a countryman, but a provincial, although (as we have seen) one who also knows the town. All this would indicate an important shift from Horace's design. Ofellus had proclaimed the virtues of plain living, and his own straitened circumstances had underlined the applicability of this advice. Bethel sets out his views as a friend; Pope is free to agree or disagree. In fact, he supports Bethel, and uses *his own situation* – rather than Bethel's – to emphasize the point. We have moved from a rhetorical to a dramatic presentation. Horace is much less implicated in his poem. He shows us Ofellus as a worthy example, who could equally be admired from afar. Pope displays himself knee deep in broccoli on his 'five acres...of rented land', grateful enough to live off 'flounders' from the Thames. This vein of comical self-belittlement runs all through the imitations; it humanizes the poetry as it catches the author seemingly unprepared to face the camera.

When Pope turns his attention to the epistles, there is not much that is obviously different in his approach. Of course, he takes over the terms of direct address used by Horace; but the slightly more mature and refined note which classical scholars find in the *Epistulae* – as against the relatively youthful *Sermones* – finds no parallel in Pope. The first epistle of the first book, which appeared in Pope's version dated '1737' (for 1738), is representative. The role of Maecenas is taken by Bolingbroke – a piece of miscasting, some would say. Yet Bolingbroke was statesman and courtier, like the Roman, a member of an ancient provincial family, a patron and a fixer. On this reading, the equivalent to the imperial court of Augustus is the Jacobite fantasy kingdom, which had centred on Rome since the Old Pretender removed there in 1719. What chiefly matters is that Pope could address Bolingbroke with just the right mixture of easy comradeship and unaffected deference. If he loses some of the philosophic weight that belongs to Horace's epistle, he yet adds a personal, quirky, sharp-witted note of his own. This is the most world-weary among the *Imitations,* and no one knew better than Pope how to make metre simulate languor:

> Now sick alike of Envy and of Praise.
> Publick too long, ah let me hide my Age!
> See modest Cibber now has left the Stage:
> Our Gen'rals now, retir'd to their Estates,
> Hang their old Trophies o'er the Garden gates,
> In Life's cool evening satiate of applause,
> Nor fond of bleeding, ev'n in BRUNSWICK's cause.
>
> (4–10)

This is a brilliant improvised excursion which takes its departure from five lines of Horace. These had utilized the metaphor of a retired gladiator: Pope compares himself to the veteran showman Colley Cibber and to the Whig generals now busy colonizing the Home Counties. (As often, Cibber's name immediately calls up in the poet a thought of the King, 'the sovereign of Brunswick'.) We are immediately out of Horace's tempo. A pained subjectivity takes over; the ancients seem to cause or mirror Pope's annoyance, where Horace had simply named an old gladiator in passing. One sees, too, how the congested line

> Hang their old Trophies o'er the Garden gates

hovers endlessly in a slow procession of syllables, time consuming and deadening.

Throughout this poem the tone is mordant and the accents urgent. A vein of Pope's best sombre comedy opens up with the mention of bodily ills (Horace applied these to Maecenas, Pope transfers them to his own 'crazy carcass'). A generalized passage in the Latin text comparing philosophy to the old discredited medicine receives a typical Popian infusion of scorn and outrage:

> Say, does thy blood rebel, thy bosom move
> With wretched Avarice, or as wretched Love?
> Know, there are Words, and Spells, which can controll
> (Between the Fits) this Fever of the soul:
> Know, there are Rhymes, which (fresh and fresh apply'd)
> Will cure the arrant'st Puppy of his Pride.
> Be furious, envious, slothful, mad or drunk,
> Slave to a Wife or Vassal to a Punk,
> A Switz, a High-dutch, or a Low-dutch Bear –
> All that we ask is but a patient Ear.
>
> (55–64)

The outlandish pun on *patient* at the end drives home the passivity of those in the hands of 'the experts' – a notion present in both Horace and Pope. Just as incisive is the concluding section, though here the imitator is translating almost literally for a time. Again there is a subtle shift. Horace presents himself as feverish and discontented, at odds with himself. Pope introduces a hint of self-pity, and also a certain teasing quality, as though daring Bolingbroke to disagree. The final compliment is apt, and yet the conclusion appears open ended – we feel that this epistle is one item selected from an ongoing correspondence. The rhetorical strategy is not that of formal satire (definitive, be done with it all): it is rather that of wheedling out a response or establishing a relationship. It is a kind of artistic statement the modern world finds impossible to make, now that 'formality' connotes stiffness and 'friendship' the absence of deep emotional involvement.

The other epistle Pope chose to imitate from the first book was the sixth. It is a good deal shorter and is less striking in the English than in its original guise, *Nil admirari*. There are several possible reasons for this dilution. Pope addressed his

poem to a young advocate named William Murray, afterwards
Lord Chief Justice Mansfield, one of the most distinguished
men of the century. We might glean from the epistle that Murray
was already cultivated, intelligent, high-minded. But as an
exemplar of 'wise indifference' he seems a little remote; his
stoic virtues freeze the writing, and his precocious dignity is
all too accurately reflected in some flabby rodomontade at the
start. In time, fortunately, Pope gets into his stride, and pro-
duces one memorable snatch of rapid characterization:

> A Man of wealth is dubb'd a Man of worth,
> Venus shall give him Form, and Anstis Birth.
> (Believe me, many a German Prince is worse,
> Who proud of Pedigree, is poor of Purse)
> His Wealth Brave Timon gloriously confounds;
> Ask'd for a Groat, he gives a hundred pounds;
> Or if three Ladies like a luckless Play,
> Takes the whole House upon the Poet's day.
>
> (81–8)

There is also a spirited passage depicting vice in high life, with
a brisk tour of 'Taverns, Stews, and Bagnio's' around the town
(118–25). But gluttony and sensuality are easy targets: it is in
the less gross temptations that Horace shows his extraordinary
point and compression (witness 11, 17–27), and Pope's rendering by comparison seems bluff, over-explicit, unconsidered.

The second book of epistles by Horace contains only two
poems. At its head stands the letter addressed to the Emperor
Augustus, who had apparently offered a good-natured com-
plaint at being excluded from the poet's dedicatees. When Pope
came to imitate this epistle in 1737, he redirected the whole
current of poetic feeling. Unable to claim that *his* sovereign
had taken an interest in his work, he adapts a Roman paean
to make of it a British lament. Every claim made on behalf
of the Emperor is forced into ironic collision with King George
Augustus, which was George II's full name. More widely, Pope
refashions a fairly gentle critique of Rome under its Caesar into
a damaging assessment of Augustan England, dominated as it

Anstis   Garter King of Arms, the leading heraldic expert of his time.

was by the Walpole administration. It is the most thorough-going rescension of Horace that he attempted.

In his Advertisement, Pope dissents from the view that the piece 'was only a *general Discourse of Poetry*; whereas it was an *Apology for the Poets,* in order to render *Augustus* more their Patron' (TE, IV, 191). In his own apology for poetry, the inadequacy of modern court patronage is vividly displayed. The 'Taste of the Town' is no longer something alien to court values: 'the People's Voice' (89) chimes in with the royal election of Colley Cibber to the bays. Fairly enough, Pope detects in Horace 'a decent Freedom' towards his Emperor; but this is greatly extended as Pope throws in one audacious reproof after another. A complete society is depicted, and yet everything is seen to flow from the top – from the King and his minions who pension the unworthy and neglect true merit. Every aspect of public conduct is shown in adverse light: where Horace can start from the Emperor's civil and military achievements, Pope drily alludes to the King's lengthy absences in Hanover and to Walpole's weak-kneed – as the Opposition saw it – foreign policy. Building on Horace's idea that Augustus, uniquely, lives to hear the praise bestowed on him by mankind, Pope suggests that George hears all too much 'present homage' even before he has done anything to deserve it (23–24). An unambiguous tribute to the nonpareil Augustus emerges in Pope heavily undercut by irony:

> Wonder of Kings! like whom, to mortal eyes
> None e'er has risen, and none e'er shall rise.
> (29–30)

Following the exordium, Pope takes up the theme of ancients and moderns, in which Horace had complained of the unjust prejudice shown against contemporary writers. Pope handles this section freely and confidently, finding apposite English equivalents for the Latin examples. He offers a judicious appraisal of earlier English poetry: warmly appreciative of true distinction, but contemptuous of the thinking by which 'works are censur'd, not as bad, but new' (116). He passes on to his famous picture of the culture of Restoration England, centring on 'the Mob of Gentlemen who wrote with Ease' (108), nicely

blending affection and disdain. The poetry, full of sudden felici-
ties, achieves that elasticity and bounce which always betray
Pope's engagement:

> No wonder then, when all was Love and Sport,
> The willing Muses were debauch'd at Court;
> On each enervate string they taught the Note
> To pant, or tremble thro' an Eunuch's throat.
> But Britain, changeful as a Child at play,
> Now calls in Princes, and now turns away.
> Now Whig, now Tory, what we lov'd we hate;
> Now all for Pleasure, now for Church and State;
> Now for Prerogative, and now for Laws;
> Effects unhappy! from a Noble cause.   (151–60)

After this come some searing denunciations of the new Georgian
climate for poetry. In Pope's scheme the role allotted to Greece
in refining rustic Latium is transferred to France. The central
passage has already been quoted (p. 9 above); it is enough
to stress here the altogether unHanoverian provenance of the
precarious literary eminence described. The epistle then turns
to the subject of comedy: Pope renders Horace with clipped
colloquial ease:

> But in known Images of life I guess
> The labour greater, as th'Indulgence less.   (284–5)

And then, by way of reflections on the uncertainty of the stage,
to a wonderful evocation of popular idiocies. We are close to
the world of *The Dunciad,* though here the note is more flippant:

> What dear delight to Britons Farce affords!
> Farce once the taste of Mobs, but now of Lords;
> (For Taste, eternal Wanderer, now flies
> From heads to ears, and now from ears to eyes.)
> The Play stands still; damn action and discourse,
> Black fly the scenes, and enter foot and horse;
> Pageants on pageants, in long order drawn,
> Peers, Heralds, Bishops, Ermin, Gold, and Lawn;
> The Champion too! and, to complete the jest,
> Old Edward's Armour beams on Cibber's breast! (310–19)

After the McLuhanesque aside on taste, note how the rhythms
of the verse enact the whole drawn-out ceremonials on stage.
Just as the action is staccato and disconnected, so are the metre
and the grammar (314–17). At the end comes Cibber, 'brazen'
as in *The Dunciad,* the very theatrical twin of Walpole in the
state. The implication is that George has been dressed in royal
garments too sumptuous by far for him.

So to the splendidly mounted conclusion, in which Horace's
reluctance to celebrate Augustus is converted by Pope into the
impossibility of anyone's fitly commemorating George. Pope
cites the line, 'Praise undeserv'd is scandal in disguise' (413),
and he leaves us in little doubt that his own preposterous rhetoric ('The Forms august of King, or conqu'ring Chief,' 391)
is wildly inappropriate to his subject. Horace ends by saying
that he would not like to be praised in bad verses which end
up as wrapping paper. Characteristically, Pope goes further:
he envisages flattery of the King as inevitably destined for the
garbage heap. It is of course the thinness of the subject, not
the poet's failings, that consigns such panegyrics to 'the rails
of Bedlam and Sohoe' (419).

The second epistle of the second book prompted one of
Pope's most individual renderings. He took as his recipient, not
like Horace a young literary aspirant, but an unnamed colonel,
a friend of Cobham and now engaged in the country life as
a gentleman farmer (see 230–9). The identity of this individual
is not significant: perhaps he is Anthony Browne, a figure
obscure enough to pass for anonymous even if he had
been named. Pope's version runs to 327 lines, half as many
again as Horace's. Its theme is the need to 'keep the equal
Measure of the Soul' (205), a resolve which apparently re-
quires that the poetic life be abjured in favour of morality or
philosophy:

> Wisdom (curse on it) will come soon or late.
>
>   (199)

The poet reflects on his own career, reasserts the seriousness
of writing, and tells a number of lively anecdotes. Most impressive, however, is a superb verse paragraph towards the end,
building on a similarly plangent section in Horace:

Heathcote himself, and such large-acred Men,
Lords of fat *E'sham,* or of Lincoln Fen,
Buy every stick of Wood that lends them heat,
But every Pullet they afford to eat.
Yet these are Wights, who fondly call their own
Half that the Dev'l o'erlooks from Lincoln Town.
The Laws of God, as well as of the Land,
Abhor, a *Perpetuity* should stand;
Estates have wings, and hang in Fortune's pow'r
Loose on the point of ev'ry wav'ring Hour;
Ready, by force, or of your own accord,
By sale, at least by death, to change their Lord.
Man? and *for ever?* Wretch! what would'st thou have?
Heir urges Heir, like Wave impelling Wave:
All vast Possessions (just the same the case
Whether you call them Villa, Park, or Chace)
Alas, my BATHURST! what will they avail?
Join *Cotswold* Hills to *Saperton's* fair Dale,
Let rising Granaries and Temples here,
There mingled Farms and Pyramids appear,
Link Towns to Towns with Avenues of Oak,
Enclose whole Downs in Walls, 'tis all a joke!
Inexorable Death shall level all,
And Trees, and Stones, and Farms, and Farmer fall.

(240–63)

This is the authentic Pope: flexibly moving from the satire of miserly landowners to the sonorous apostrophe, 'my Bathurst!' and then to the muted conclusion. The poet visualizes a social process as a cosmic cycle; he relates the order of nature to towns, parks, villas, granaries, where Milton would have invoked celestial bodies, but the effect is very much the same. There are few finer examples of Pope's mature skill than this epistle. It shows him enlisting imagery, rhythm, proverbial echoes, topical allusions and moral exempla to a coherent purpose. It is the greatness of Pope that he can dramatize an economic or social theme, reveal its deep ironic implications, and yet convey an intensely vivid awareness of the here and now. Augustan England is revealed as a palimpsest of eternity.

The *Epilogue to the Satires* came out in two separate parts in 1738 – the first part indeed originally bore that year as its title. It makes a worthy culmination to the series: Dialogue I exhibits a wide range of poetic moods, from a tetchy and thin-skinned depression to the lofty despair of the conclusion. A token 'friend' is present as interlocutor, goading Pope into self-defence or combative retort. Freed from Horace, after an opening allusion to one of the satires, Pope yet writes even now under the aegis of the Roman poet. He indeed offers up the patently weak justification of his writings that they are 'all from Horace' (7); and after his friend has deflected this line of argument, he stands ironically 'exposed', unable to conceal the directness of his assault on Walpole. The rhetorical strategy is to imply that Horace's day is done: corruption has gone so far that the 'sly, polite, insinuating stile' (19) is no longer sufficient corrective. Gloom at the turn of political events suffuses the *Epilogue*. A few years earlier, it had seemed possible that the coalition of Patriots might establish a solid Opposition to the ministry. It had numbered in its ranks Bolingbroke, Pulteney, Chesterfield, William Pitt the elder and Lyttelton, and attracted a bevy of literary men in its support. But Bolingbroke brought back from his exile no power base to match his expansive polemical instincts; Pulteney was notoriously undependable, and broke away in the end; Pitt was only just beginning his career; Lyttelton was a second-rate man of affairs; whilst the clutch of epics and dramas *à clef* was no substitute for effective political action from the litterateurs. They would have done better to compile broadside ballads than their elaborate allegories of the Walpole machine – besides the fact that some, like Henry Fielding, eventually came round to the minister's side. Chance after chance was lost, notably the crisis precipitated by the unpopular Excise Bill in 1733. And by 1738 it was clear to all that, however Walpole was to be dislodged, it could not be through the hands of the splintered Patriot group. When he finally succumbed in 1742, it was no more than a palace revolution, engineered and exploited by Whig pragmatists in his own image.

Out of this disillusion Pope constructs a fierce, exclamatory poem of protest. The friend's anodyne interjections contrast

abruptly with Pope's own contemptuous outbursts against
wheeler-dealers in the state:

> Ye Gods! shall *Cibber*'s Son, without rebuke,
> Swear like a Lord? or *Rich* out-whore a Duke?
> A Fav'rite's Porter with his Master vie,
> Be brib'd as often, and as often lie?
> Shall *Ward* draw Contracts with a Statesman's skill?
> Or *Japhet* pocket, like his Grace, a Will?
> Is it for *Bond* or *Peter* (paltry Things!)
> To pay their Debts or keep their Faith like Kings!
>
> (115–23)

We are close to Swift here – not just in the bitterness of these
comments, but in the quality of surprise, as Pope affects to
take it for granted that graft is a matter of course in the highest
echelons of society. Then comes one of the greatest passages
in Pope, setting out the unequal contest between 'Virtue' (political probity, 'Opposition' values) and 'Vice' (the Walpole system). In his most elevated manner, Pope designs a baroque
setpiece to portray the triumph of vice:

> Let *Greatness* own her, and she's mean no more:
> Her Birth, her Beauty, Crowds and Courts confess,
> Chaste Matrons praise her, and grave Bishops bless:
> In golden Chains the willing World she draws,
> And hers the Gospel is, and hers the Laws:
> Mounts the Tribunal, lifts her scarlet head,
> And sees pale Virtue carted in her stead!
> Lo! at the Wheels of her Triumphal Car,
> Old *England*'s Genius, rough with many a Scar,
> Dragg'd in the Dust! his Arms hang idly round,
> His Flag inverted trails along the ground!
>
> (144–55)

The iconography here calls up a recollection of the Whore of
Babylon (*Revelations,* xvii), and there is probably an allusion
to Walpole's mistress Molly Skerrett.[5] But the power of the allegory is more general: it derives from the intensely realized detail,
the trenchant accuracy of the wording (many expressions, like

'Old England', have a political cant meaning), and the magnificent control of sound, rhythm and syntax leading up to a perfect climax.

There is nothing of comparable majesty in the second dialogue. What there is, however, stands up by itself: a 'bitter and proud affirmation'[6] of the need for plain-spoken satire, and of Pope's own integrity:

> Yes, I am proud; I must be proud to see
> Men not afraid of God, afraid of me:
> Safe from the Bar, the Pulpit, and the Throne,
> Yet touch'd and sham'd by *Ridicule* alone....
> Ye tinsel Insects! whom a Court maintains,
> That counts your Beauties only by your Stains,
> Spin all your Cobwebs o'er the Eye of Day!
> The Muse's swing shall brush you all away:
> All his Grace preaches, all his Lordship sings,
> All that makes Saints of Queens, and Gods of Kings,
> All, all but Truth, drops dead-born from the Press,
> Like the last Gazette, or the last Address.
>
> (208–11, 220–7)

This sublimely arrogant gesture of dismissal has behind it a lofty contempt – Pope could be as vain as the next man, but his grandiloquent language here proceeds from a public (if not quite impersonal) sense of outrage:

> Truth guards the Poet, sanctifies the line,
> And makes Immortal, Verse as mean as mine.
>
> (246–7)

As in his early poems, Pope is asserting the tenacity of art. The satirist undertakes to 'rowze the Watchmen of the Publick Weal' (217), and so acts as the conscience of the nation. We need not agree with Pope's appraisal of the Walpole ministry (for it is certainly far from objective); but we can all feel the energy and confidence which such a concept of his vocation lent to Pope's writing. Despair may destroy the working politician; it can be the making of a poet.

It is natural that attention should have been given in recent years to the two imitations of Donne, since the huge growth

of interest in the earlier writer. One must not bring the wrong
kind of expectation to these works, however. The Augustan age
valued Donne, if it did so at all, for his quaintness; and it read
into his satires a cheerful clumsiness which our more reverential
eyes are unlikely to discern. Pope attempted only two of the
five surviving pieces. The fourth satire was rendered anonymously in 1733. It was joined in a collected volume of *Works*
in 1735 by the second satire, which Pope had originally
attempted some twenty years earlier – the published version is
thoroughly recast and illustrates the changes which had gone
on in Pope's style in the meantime. In general Pope seeks to
add smoothness, connection and clarity to Donne's text; both
at the local level – in syntax – and in the wider organization
of verse paragraphs, he introduces order and sequentiality.
Donne's *Satyres* have been called 'long outbursts, impassioned
soliloquies'.[7] Pope substitutes argument for rhetoric, controlled
energy for outright vehemence. But it is certainly not a matter
of reducing Donne to a timidly 'correct' level. In his own fashion
Pope is just as racy, imaginative and realistic as Donne. The
fourth satire in particular affords him plenty of opportunities
to add personal and topical detail without losing the thread
of Donne's case:

> Loth to enrich me with too quick Replies,
> By little, and by little, drops his Lies.
> Meer *Household Trash*! of Birth-nights, Balls and Shows,
> More than ten *Holingsheds,* or *Halls,* or *Stows.*
> When the *Queen* frown'd, or smil'd, he knows; and what
> A subtle Minister may make of that?
> Who sins with whom? who got his Pension *Rug*
> Or quicken'd a Reversion by a *Drug?*
> Whose Place is *quarter'd out,* three Parts in four,
> And whether to a Bishop, or a Whore?
> Who, having lost his Credit, pawn'd his Rent,
> Is therefore fit to have a *Government?*
> Who in the *Secret,* deals in Stocks secure,
> And cheats th'unknowing Widow, and the Poor?

Rug   safely

> Who makes a *Trust,* or *Charity,* a Job,
> And gets an Act of Parliament to rob?
> Why *Turnpikes* rise, and now no Cit, nor Clown
> Can *gratis* see the *Country,* or the *Town?*
> Shortly no Lads shall *chuck,* or Lady *vole,*
> But some excising Courtier will have Toll.
>
> (128–47)

The idea of 'paying toll' is actually present in Donne; but Pope
has marvellously reanimated the expression by reference to contemporary scandals like the fraudulent Charitable Corporation,
the unpopular turnpike trusts and the notorious Excise scheme.
As always, the effect of the social detail is *poetic* as well as moral.
There is a harsh paradox in the use to which the noble abstrac-
tions 'trust' and 'charity' are put: to such a point have we come,
Pope implies, that jobbery sullies our finest ideals and the names
by which we call them. This is a process we see delineated
throughout the Horatian poems. It took a great master of words
to do all this: to reveal the state of society by making language
misapply itself. Just as George Augustus, together with his court,
fails to be Augustan, so honour declines to be honourable:

> See, all our Nobles begging to be Slaves!
> See, all our Fools aspiring to be Knaves!
> The Wit of Cheats, the Courage of a Whore,
> Are what ten thousand envy and adore.
> All, all look up, with reverential Awe,
> On Crimes that scape, or triumph o'er the Law:
> While Truth, Worth, Wisdom, daily they decry –
> 'Nothing is Sacred now but Villany.'
>
> Yet may this Verse (if such a Verse remain)
> Show there was one who held it in disdain.
>
> (*IH*, Epilogue I, 163–72)

The verse does, indeed, remain. And its brutal exposure of the
gap between profession and practice survives to tell the tale.

Chuck   play chuck-farthing
Vole   take the tricks in ombre

CHAPTER EIGHT

The empire of dulness

The Dunciad is a comic poem. The fact is worth stressing at the outset: solemn scholarship has long overweighted this work with more than Scriblerian owlishness. Marshall McLuhan has apotheosized *The Dunciad* as the supreme critique of print as a stupefying drug. 'The last book', he states, 'proclaims the metamorphic power of mechanically applied knowledge as a stupendous parody of the Eucharist.' It has to do with 'the translation or reduction of diverse modes into a single mode of homogenized things.'[1] Other critics sound almost as portentous. Yet it surely is wrong to inflate the 'ideas' content of the work, if by this means we diminish its vivacity and fun. Pope has given us a huge insult, an insolent reproof of the long line of his detractors. It is a giant raspberry of a satire, making its points through outrageous cheek as well as subtle literary conversions. As James Sutherland has argued, Pope's personal vulnerability did not spill into the poetry: the anguish may have been real, but the bitterness merely set his comic invention to work.[2] It is equally important to remember that this *is* a poem, using the full resources at Pope's command – rhythm, sound effects, syntax, metaphor, allusion and so on. *The Dunciad* is a marvellous feat of linguistic virtuosity; the English tongue has rarely been stretched in so many directions. The boisterous busyness of the dunces is matched by the daring exuberance of the words. Puns and paradoxes abound; on these lexical playfields a term like 'Dulness' can refer now to a character, now to an abstract quality, then again it can be made to hover indefinitely in space, neither quite concrete and referential nor wholly allegorical.

A further warning. It is too easily assumed that the conclusion of *The Dunciad* represents Pope's last despairing word. But most of the poem as we have it dates from the 1720s, before the gloom of the Tory satirists had closed in on the bright Scriblerus hoaxers. Even the famous lines at the very end, or most of them, belong to the first version of 1728, though here they form part of the vision of the prophetic ghost of Settle. Nor is the last book, added in 1742, uniformly bleak. Pope can single out a few contemporaries of merit (e.g. IV, 167–70), and his tone is often near to playful. In fact, as with *Gulliver's Travels* and *The Beggar's Opera,* the satirist is able to share an experience of the most intensely unpleasant kind, and yet at the same time communicates a feeling of exhilarating and spontaneous glee.

This is a direct consequence of the mock-heroic method. The form permits a writer special licence: he can employ a destructive and even offensive manner of speaking, shielded by the decorous coat of mock epic style. Thus the account of the pissing contest in Book II avoids embarrassment by reason of the patent disproportion of the words to the things:

> The Goddess then: 'Who best can send on high
> The salient spout, far-streaming to the sky;
> His be yon Juno of majestic size,
> With cow-like udders, and with ox-like eyes....'
> Not so from shameless Curl? impetuous spread
> The stream, and smoking flourish'd o'er his head.
> So (fam'd like thee for turbulence and horns)
> Eridanus his humble fountain scorns;
> Thro' half the heav'ns he pours th'exalted urn;
> His rapid waters in their passage burn.
>
> (II, 161–4, 179–84)

The irrelevant beauty of certain turns of phrase cheat our expectations; we are induced to feel that the poet is indulging his bent for fanciful comparison, and so 'pass', without our usual instinctive censorship, the aggressive implications against Curll – that he is ready to make a public exhibition of himself, that he suffers from the clap (hence the 'burning' urine), that he spreads his dirt all over the place, and so on. The parody of heroic idiom *seems* to mitigate the fierceness of the attack. But really it allows all the more venom to get by without disturbing the surface polish of the description.

Mock-heroic is only one of a number of strands in the fabric of *The Dunciad.* Sticking to round figures, we can isolate ten elements in the imaginative design – they may be technical devices or what we generally call 'themes', but they all serve a single vision of triumphant dulness.

(1)   Let us start with mock-heroic, whose stylistic consequences we have just touched on. This element connects the poem with Dryden's *Mac Flecknoe,* another poem describing the succession of one bad poet to another, and likewise set on the fringes of the City of London. It also corresponds to the layout of *The Rape of the Lock.* But in that case generalized allusion to the conventions of epic had been predominant. Now Pope uses orthodox mock epic more sparingly, reserving his parody of particular effects for a critical moment – e.g. the sudden absurd reference to Minerva when the goddess yawns (IV, 606, note). 'The mockery of the epic form is there; but in the *Dunciad* Pope's primary concern is not to write mock epic, but to make use of that form to satirize his enemies.'[3]

(2)   There are however two important exceptions, where Pope deliberately sustains a current of allusion to particular epics. There is first of all Virgil's *Aeneid,* which was in many respects the most congenial of all heroic poems to the eighteenth century. Of course, the relationship is a devious and ironic one: it is first announced by the pedantic commentator, Martinus Scriblerus, in his prosy introduction to the work:

> ...the Action of the Dunciad is the Removal of the Imperial seat of Dulness from the City to the polite world; as that of the Aeneid is the Removal of the empire of *Troy* to *Latium.*

> (TE, V, 51)

The poem, then, is dynastic in conception; it has to do with the progress of an empire, and indeed the imperial theme is taken up more than once – explicitly in the Argument to Book III, which refers to 'the past triumphs of the Empire of Dulness' (TE, V, 319), and more pervasively in the text of this book (III, 73–138). Professor Aubrey Williams has shown how the traditional idea of London as Troy-novant was reshaped by Pope to bring special aptness to this adaptation of the Virgilian myth.[4] Williams also demonstrates that Pope utilized another well-established genre, the 'progress piece', and another bit of contemporary thinking, the notion of *translatio studii,* to fill out this

legend.[5] To be blunt, the idea of a historical spread of civilization from one age or nation to another is only a crude sub-
anthropology, Renaissance fol-de-rols to conceal ignorance and
dignify the present. But it served Pope's purposes well enough.
His main reason for alluding to the *Aeneid* was to set up this
counter-image of a heroic quest to discover a kingdom: against
this he measures the foundation of the empire of Dulness.

(3)   More fitful use is made of the greatest Renaissance epic,
Milton's *Paradise Lost*. The new King Dunce is constantly presented as another Satan; Milton's figures of Sin and Death are
recalled by the operations of Dulness. Again Williams's book
is most helpful. He argues that Pope injects a conscious devilry
into his creation by stirring in our minds recollections of Milton:
'By no other means could Pope have so readily revealed the
evil implicit in duncery as he conceived it than by his parody
of *Paradise Lost*, the metaphoric alliance of duncery with diabo-
lism.' Further, Williams believes that Pope constructed an anti-
theology, 'an inverse paradigm of creation', where the Supreme
being is an image of nullity and destruction.[6] But even if this
is so, the *structural* implications are less important than in the
case of the *Aeneid*. It is the action or 'fable' of Virgil's poem
that underlies *The Dunciad*, whereas it is the religious and imaginative design of *Paradise Lost* that Pope invokes as a grisly
contrast to the unholy mess which constitutes the spirit of
Dulness:

> Lo! thy dread Empire! CHAOS! is restor'd;
> Light dies before thy uncreating word.   (IV, 653–4)

Christianity, and all civilization, has had its work undone: pri-
meval darkness reassumes the land.

(4)   In contrast to these traditional elements, with their
memories of a noble past, we turn to a group of starkly contemporary themes. Most of them root the poem in a recent past
and in a closely adjacent setting. Where the epic allusions (despite their mocking function) had opened out the design in
time and space, these components serve to fix *The Dunciad* in
a localized and in some respects almost parochial situation.
In fact, the four next elements we shall look at bear specifically
on London and on eighteenth-century conditions.

Most specific of all is the parody of the Lord Mayor's Day junketings, notably in Book II. Aubrey Williams remarks that 'there are many remarkable similarities in the routes followed by the two processions [Lord Mayor's and dunces']. ...Even the divergences appear to realize, in symbolic fashion, the mayoral journey'. He adds that 'the imaginative significance of the geographical movements in the poem remains clear'. That is, the dunces represent the encroachment of City powers upon the 'polite' quarter of the town, the West End. The progress is seen less as a piece of municipal pageantry than as an arrogant assertion of the dominance of the City and the moneyed interest over the more humane values (as the Tory satirists affected to believe) of Westminster. The absurd duncely games are held near the junction of the Strand and Drury Lane. This was a district where playhouses and coffee rooms abounded; booksellers and printers (prominent in the games) had long colonized the Strand and Fleet Street. Indeed almost every stopping place on the dunces' itinerary – almost every locality mentioned in Book II – has strong links with the book trade: Chancery Lane (II, 263), St Paul's (II, 346), the Temple (II, 98) and Ludgate (II, 359) figure in many an imprint. Thus the stationers as well as the writers are implicated in the deluge of bookmaking; and they contribute to what Williams terms 'the encroachment of literary dulness on Westminster'.[7]

In the first version of the poem, we are even told the precise Lord Mayor whose festivities the dunces share:

> 'Twas on the day, when Thorold, rich and grave,
> Like Cimon triumph'd, both on land and wave.
>
> (A, I, 83–4)

Pope's note reads, 'Sir *George Thorold* Lord Mayor of *London*, in the Year 1720. The procession of a Lord Mayor is made partly by land, and partly by water'. In the revised *Dunciad,* the personal name was replaced by an asterisk, and a note inserted finding fault with the identification previously 'foisted in'. There is a mere joking pedanticism; Thorold was largely forgotten by the 1740s, and Pope had no reason to cling on to his presence. But for all that it is certain that the action *was* originally placed in November 1719, when Thorold took office. Pope wanted the events to begin 'in the last reign' (TE, V, 205), not just for reasons of politic evasion, but in order to reinforce his running dialectic of *handing on office* – Settle passes on the torch to the new King (either Theobald or Cibber), whilst George the Second succeeds his father in Hanoverian torpor. This last event, which took place in June 1727, was of course highly topical when *The Dunciad* first appeared. On one level, then, the Lord Mayor's celebrations may be a thinly veiled metaphor to hint at the paraphernalia of a royal succession – always a nervous juncture in that era :

> This important point of time our Poet has chosen, as the Crisis of the Kingdom of *dulness,* who thereupon decrees to remove her imperial seat from the City, and over-spread the other parts of the Town : to which great Enterprize all things being now ripe, she calls the Hero of this Poem.
>
> (A, I, 88, note)

The phrase about things being ripe for 'this great Enterprize' echoes the language of dynastic plotting : the Jacobite attempts to dislodge George I, most obviously. So the succession of Dulness is confirmed, with a subliminal suggestion that bolder men would have resisted George II's peaceful progression to the throne.

(5)   Less narrowly, the poem gives us a picture of urban disorder. It images London life as a continual experience of buffeting, overcrowding, stench and squalor. *The Dunciad* is perhaps the first great literary embodiment of a familiar modern theme – the pressures of city living. Of course, writers like Ben Jonson and Dekker, and for that matter Defoe, had already contrived significant fictions out of town life. But Pope was more radically innovative : he somehow apprehended the electric quality of urban existence, the kind of thing we associate today with New York, and rendered this threat and excitement in the texture of his poem. He seems indeed to have intuited the course of subsequent history. The uproarious goings on of his duncely troop prefigure in an astonishing way modes of popular protest which were scarcely known in Pope's day, but which came to a head with riots later in the century – those of the Spitalfields weavers in the 1750s and 1760s, the Wilkes trouble in 1768,

and above all the Gordon riots in 1780. The point is not that Pope is directly portraying the dunces as populist rioters. It is rather that he drew on his deepest fund of creative energy to build up a 'myth of social disorder',[8] and in some miraculous fashion his own consciousness of the city included protest and insurrection, as well as noise, poverty and crime – even though, in sober fact, urban development had scarcely yet proceeded to quite such a neurotic pitch. Pope, in a sense, collaborates imaginatively with history. He connected crowding and violence, by pure poetic logic, and thus anticipated the findings of later sociology:

> 'And oh! (he cry'd) what street, what lane but knows,
> Our purgings, pumpings, blankettings, and blows?'
>
> (II, 153–4)

The plosive alliteration of the style enacts the blind collision of blunt objects which the poem sets in motion. The grammar, like the enveloping drama, takes the space away from between things, and unresistingly they beat into one another.

(6) Closely allied is the depiction of Grub Street. Most of the actors in his fable are denizens of the place, literally or otherwise. Most of the dunces mentioned by name are professional writers, characterized sufficiently by their various productions. In Book I, in the mock-heroic way, authors are seen chiefly as physical objects – volumes in a library, or printed sheets consigned to undignified tasks, Later in the poem, the writers do take on a personal identity; but they are always liable to revert to the primitive sludge that is Dulness:

> Now thousand tongues are heard in one large din:
> The Monkey-mimics rush discordant in;
> 'Twas chatt'ring, grinning, mouthing, jabb'ring all,
> And Noise and Norton, Brangling and Breval,
> Dennis and Dissonance, and captious Art,
> And Snip-snap short, and Interruption smart....
>
> (II, 235–40)

In just a few places, Pope's attitude is complicated by a suspicion of fellow-feeling: some hint of sympathy creeps into the description of the aged critic (II, 283–90), and Pope knows too much about some of the characters, e.g. John Dennis, to be able to treat them in a wholly impersonal way. Nevertheless the writers are chiefly significant within *The Dunciad* as a collectivity, rather than as individuals. The fact that we do not recognize their names today is part of the joke. Plenty of contemporaries would have been pushed to put a face to Thomas Foxton:

> Lo Bond and Foxton, ev'ry nameless name.   (A, III, 151)

Such hacks often wrote anonymously or under a disguised name; but Pope suggests that they have no need to conceal their identity, since nobody cares about them in any case. Most of the stationers were perhaps better known; an eighteenth-century title page usually proclaims the bookseller's name, if no one else's. But the same point holds. If the reader has no idea who 'Mears, Warner, Wilkins' are, that reinforces the satire; their function is to be nobodies:

> Three wicked imps, of her own Grubstreet choir,
> She deck'd like Congreve, Addison, and Prior;
> Mears, Warner, Wilkins run: delusive thought!
> Breval, Bond, Besaleel, the varlets caught.
> Curl stretches after Gay, but Gay is gone,
> He grasps an empty Joseph for a John:
> So Proteus, hunted in a nobler shape,
> Became, when seiz'd, a puppy, or an ape.
>
> (II, 123–30)

It does not matter who is who. Literary production has become a standardized process of fraud and piracy; commercial writing could indeed be performed by a fabricated identikit hack, a phantom who has to be allocated a name like More (II, 35–50).

One of the changes introduced into the poem in 1743 has passed relatively unobserved. The 'Cave of Poverty and Poetry' (A, I, 32; B, I, 33) is removed from its former location, an old clothes market Rag Fair, which lay near the Tower of London. It is now set down 'Close to those walls where Folly holds her throne', i.e. in the environs of the madhouse, Bedlam. Of course this confirms a pervasive body of allusions to insanity. But it is at least possible that Pope had some explicit London landmark in mind. His editor Warburton wrote that 'The cell of poor Poetry is here very properly represented as a little *unendowed Hall* in the neighbourhood of the Magnific College of Bedlam.... For there cannot be a plainer indication of madness than in men's persisting to starve themselves and offend the public by scribling...' (TE, V, 271). This comment has been interpreted to refer to Sion College, an Anglican establishment just inside the old City walls. But Sion College had no particular reputation for scribbling; and it seems much more likely that Pope and Warburton had in mind an equally adjacent point on the map – Grub Street, the historic and legendary abode of authors. This ran north–south a stone's throw away from Bedlam. It had often been linked with the madhouse, and there was a satiric point in viewing its inhabitants as lunatics – something that is hardly true of Sion College. It was commonly described as a 'Seminary' (e.g. in the pro-Pope *Grub-street Journal* in 1731), and Dr Arbuthnot had even used the image of a University. Thus when Warburton in the same note calls the college 'the surest Seminary to supply those learned Walls with Professors', he was employing the Scriblerian lexicon – 'O *Grub-street*,' cries Arbuthnot, 'thou fruitful Nursery of towering Genius's!' Such an application would lend force to the entire poem. By placing the nerve centre of Dulness in Grub Street, Pope could cement the imaginative design of *The Dunciad* and make it (what it was implicitly from the start) an epic of scribbling humanity.[9]

(7) There is a parallel thread of meaning concerned with Smithfield, which lay a few hundred yards to the west. Here we get rather more help from the text. The first couplet of the poem is enough:

> Books and the Man I sing, the first who brings
> The Smithfield Muses to the Ear of Kings.
>
> (A, I, 1–2)

Martinus Scriblerus fills this out in a convenient fashion; as often, his laborious pedantry supplies an important insight despite itself:

...[the action of the poem is] the introduction of the lowest

diversion of the rabble in *Smithfield* to be the entertainment
of the court and town.

(TE, V, 51)

In other words, the 'Smithfield muses' – low spectacle and fairground farce – are supplanting the serious drama. Court
patronage is now bestowed on the lowest, not the highest,
reaches of art. In present-day terms we might say that this is
a kind of treachery of the clerks, though we may be less willing
to condemn the adoption by an élite of fashionable popular
culture – it is something we witness all the time nowadays. But
for men of Pope's habit of mind, it was to renege on the noblest
duties of an educated man. It meant defiling the theatre: pollut-
ing a sacred fountain.

Pope appended this note to his opening invocation of the
Smithfield muse: '*Smithfield* is the place where Bartholomew
Fair was kept, whose Shews, Machines, and Dramatical Entertainments, formerly only agreeable to the Taste of the Rabble,
were, by the Hero of this Poem and others of equal Genius,
brought to the Theatres of Covent-Garden, Lincolns-inn-
Fields, and the Hay-Market, to be the reigning Pleasures of
the Court and Town. This happened in the Reigns of King
George I, and II. See Book 3.' In that third book, we see many
references to elaborate stage spectacle: men like John Rich,
the impresario at Lincoln's Inn, had specialized in gaudy harlequinades and absurd eye-catching shows – we recall the lines
in the *Epistle to Augustus*, quoted on p. 95, indicating how taste
'now flies / From heads to ears, and now from ears to eyes'.
The original King Dunce, Lewis Theobald, had contributed to
this sub-literature with his garishly presented *Rape of Proserpine*
(1727). His pantomime *Perseus and Andromeda* was produced as
a fairground puppet show in 1730, just too late to rate a mention
in the first *Dunciad,* though not to underline its meaning. His
successor as arch-dunce, Colley Cibber, had a ballad opera
acted at Bartholomew Fair in 1729; his son and daughter had
been acting there for a number of years. Both men, therefore,
could reasonable be associated with the vogue for the *théâtre
des machines,* though there was as we shall see an even stronger
connecting link available. It should also be noted that Pope

treats opera as a symptom of the same disease (IV, 45–70). This may have been unjust, though Pope had Addison's amusing papers as a precedent (*Spectator* Nos. 5, 18 and 31). To the humanist mind all sound without sense was to be deplored, and all showmanship suspect. It helped, too, that men like Rich and the operatic impresario Heidegger could plausibly be aligned with the great political 'manager', Robert Walpole. Hence the rise of a star system – with the rival operatic queens and the great castrato Farinelli – could be seen as an effete showbusiness culture to parallel the jobbing administration – the opera audience hum, snore and yawn (IV, 59–60) just as the political nation falls into heavy slumber at the climax of the poem (IV, 607–18). Popular culture, in other words, is one of the opiates of Dulness.[10]

(8) We have already come across several hints of the presence of politics in *The Dunciad*. In general the theme is handled more deviously than in the *Imitations of Horace*. Nevertheless, there is a strong current of feeling which indicts Dulness as a political phenomenon. Very early on we get a nudge in this direction with the line, 'Still Dunce the second reigns like Dunce the first' (I, 6). This survives in the revised text, and takes more point from the enduring capacity of George II to cling on to life (he was to survive Pope a further sixteen years). There is no doubt that the soporific Palinurus of IV, 614, is Walpole, and Pope must have in mind the state of naval and military unpreparedness with which Britain undertook the War of Jenkins' Ear in 1739, a commitment Walpole persistently but unavailingly opposed. Other hints are less palpable: there are a number of places where we are inclined to suppose that 'the Queen' is not just Dulness, but also Caroline of Anspach, consort of George II (see for example: I, 214; IV, 20; IV, 280; IV, 506). For the most part Pope seems to be gunning for the court through its minion, the appointed laureate Cibber. It is one of the major strokes in the replacement of Theobald: for whatever his faults, the original King had never been a court favourite. With Cibber enthroned in his place, the poem has much more room to do its political work.

(9) A little aslant from all these matters, *The Dunciad* is a standing rebuke to pedantry. Its own form mimics the top-heavy

accretion of pseudo-scholarship upon slender texts. The endless delaying tactics of the preliminaries recall Swift's *Tale of a Tub*, another anti-book which makes its own envelope a parodic weapon. Equally, the laborious footnotes impugn over-meticulous attention to verbal detail even as they slily cap Pope's innuendoes. Scriblerus is backed by the fine invention of 'Ricardus Aristarchus', who turns up in another guise within the poem (IV, 201–74) and again with his busy but misconceived annotations. Through the person of Aristarchus Pope makes his most direct attack on the arrogance of scholars who 'Made Horace dull, and humbled Milton's strains' (IV, 212). However, this is supported by the entire construction of *The Dunciad* after the appearance of its instant Variorum text. The new world of Dulness is one where wits earn that name by mincing standard authors to bits (IV, 119–34). Scholarship diminishes instead of preserving; its insulation of words from things makes it uncreative, anti-humanist, an education for Dulness.

(10)   Finally, *The Dunciad* is a giant-sized joke – an extension of the Scriblerian 'squib' to the fullest dimensions of high art. Its appearance marked an *event*: the work was carefully mounted with all Pope's devious ingenuity. As Emrys Jones has well said, describing the sudden presence of this extraordinary construct in the England of George II:

> Just as the Lilliputians one day found the sleeping man-giant Gulliver within their kingdom, so Pope's contemporaries can be imagined as discovering this strange offensive object, lying in a public place like an enemy weapon or a ponderous missile: essentially not a set of abstract verbal statements but a thing, to be walked around and examined, interpreted, and possibly dealt with.[11]

This is a brilliant evocation of the thinginess of the poem, together with its hostile potential and its disquieting denseness. *The Dunciad Variorum* of 1729 was planned all along; and only when the full apparatus is present, as Jones says, is the 'solid three-dimensional' quality of the poem truly apparent. To amplify his comparison, one might say that *The Dunciad* emanated overnight like the wooden horse in Troy – an episode by no means distant from the poem's concerns. For years after its publication, the poem seeped out a trickle of combative meanings – you could never leave it alone in the bland assurance that it had done its work. This is partly a result of Pope's well-organized espionage system. He had his man in Grub Street, the extravagant bohemian figure Richard Savage, who is best known today as the subject of a vivid biography by Samuel Johnson. But the rich allusive fabric of the verse is another factor. *The Dunciad* stores up innuendo in diction and imagery; when the time is ripe, the damaging details steal out and reveal themselves. It is retaliation by art.[12]

These separate strands in the work might promote over-elaboration. But in all sorts of ways Pope manages to make one level of meaning assist another. For example, the Lord Mayor's procession neatly dovetails with the Virgilian parody; the critique of Cibber (showman, hack and court nominee) is underpinned by allusions to Milton's Satan. Moreover there is a brilliant piece of casting which serves to unite several components in the design. This was the choice of Elkanah Settle to take over the role of ghostly father figure – that is, the function of Anchises in the *Aeneid*. Through Settle's agency the poem is anchored in the tradition of *Mac Flecknoe* – he had actually had his brushes with Dryden and with Thomas Shadwell, the original of Mac Flecknoe. He was a true denizen of Grub Street, a Londoner through and through, and one with a direct interest in City ceremonial. His career made him the perfect representative of old Dulness, ready to pass on its mysteries to the new breed of dunce.

This aptness is particularly striking in the case of *The Dunciad Variorum*. In the Argument to Book I, we are told that the King Dunce is found 'apprehending' the decline of the empire of Dulness owing to 'the old age of the present monarch *Settle*' (TE, V, 54). Actually Settle was still alive as late as 1719, when the action is set; he died before the poem was written. He enters the poem proper at line 87:

> Now Night descending, the proud scene was o'er,
> But liv'd, in Settle's numbers, one day more.

It might seem impossible to augment the cruelty; but the note lays on further indignities, as well as supplying some necessary facts:

> *Settle* was alive at this time, and Poet to the City of *London*. His office was to compose yearly panegyricks upon the Lord Mayors, and Verses to be spoken in the Pageants.

Settle was indeed the last City Poet – a nicely inaccurate term, in that the job involved mounting costly production numbers as well as writing panegyrical verse (Settle had an unhappy fondness for titles like *Augusta Triumphans*). Later in the poem Pope releases more information:

> *Settle,* like most Party-writers, was very uncertain in his political principles. He was employ'd to hold the pen in the *Character* of a *Popish successor,* but afterwards printed his *Narrative* on the contrary side. He had managed the Ceremony of a famous Pope-burning on *Nov.* 17, 1680: then became a Trooper of King *James*'s army at *Hounslow-heath*: After the Revolution he kept a Booth at *Bartlemew-fair,* where in his Droll call'd St. *George for England,* he acted in his old age in a Dragon of green leather of his own invention. He was at last taken into the Charterhouse, and there dyed, aged about 60 years.

> (A, III, 281, note)

Here we have in a short space a number of themes: politics, Grub Street writing, Smithfield droll-making, organizing demonstrations, and so on. Enough by itself, we may think, to equip him for his role.

But there is a deeper level of implication. It happens that Settle had enjoyed his greatest triumph with an opera on the 'fate of Troy', which was revamped for the fairground audience under the title *The Siege of Troy*. As such it met with great success at Smithfield from 1707 onwards. This was indeed the archetypal droll, full of fantastic machinery and remarkable scenery. The decor is said to have cost the fairground stallholder a huge sum of money. This 'expensive entertainment' laid out all its funds upon a feast for the eye, with garish transformation scenes and spectacular costumes. It was still popular in the 1730s, when Hogarth showed it playing at Southwark Fair in his famous print. Now the point is that Settle is seen in *The Dunciad* as the forlorn defender of Troy, the metaphoric equivalent of Grub Street. In real life it was he who had devised the fall of Troy in its most prominent dramatic statement – as opera and then as droll, two notable expressions of Dulness in the satire. So Settle had in a sense 'rais'd from Booths to Theatre' (A, III, 301) the legend of Troy, whose recital by Virgil lies behind the entire *Dunciad*. It helped that he had attempted his own heroic tragedies on exotic themes, and that he had actually collaborated on theatrical work with the original King of the dunces, Lewis Theobald. But the central fact is that his vision of the new empire of Dulness, which forms the climax of the three-book version, draws on a vein of dramatic spectacle he had himself made his own at Bartholomew Fair. His picture of the sacking of Troy brings irresistibly to mind the lines Pope gives him in *The Dunciad*:

> All sudden, Gorgons hiss and Dragons glare,
> And ten-horn'd fiends and Giants rush to war.
> Hell rises, Heav'n descends, and dance on Earth,
> Gods, imps, and monsters, music, rage, and mirth,
> A fire, a jig, a battle, and a ball,
> Till one wide Conflagration swallows all.
>
> (A, III, 231–6)

Settle was no pedant, and left Milton well alone. Otherwise there is scarcely any major theme of the poem which does not implicate him in some degree. Even with the course of time and the changes Pope made to the text, he remains a singularly apt choice. A City poet from Grub Street, active in civil broils, and politically suspect, by whose hand the Virgilian legend had been acted out in the Smithfield fashion – it is almost too neat to be true.

* * * * *

Two interrelated problems have chiefly exercised commentators on *The Dunciad*. A third issue has recently come to the fore. It is possible to read the poem without being unduly disturbed by any of these matters, such are the *brio* and invention Pope commands. But since competent students, not unsympathetic to Pope, have been perplexed or divided by these points, they deserve some attention.

First, there is the alleged lack of action. This is sometimes linked with the charge that the fourth book is imperfectly assimilated, and tends to stand out as a powerful but inorganic afterthought. The most powerful case along these lines has been drawn up by Ian Jack, who misses any 'consistent following-out of the mock-heroic idea', as against the sure handling of structure in *The Rape of the Lock*.[13] Defenders have not been lacking; but it is perhaps fair to say that no fully adequate reply has been made directly to Jack's complaints of a failure to observe literary decorum. For example, Howard Erskine-Hill's excellent study of 'The "New World" of Pope's *Dunciad*' attempts to outflank Jack, rather than meet his precise points; it argues that the scope of the poem is widened and amplified through a logical development of 'dulness' – in other words, that the consistency is not that of thoroughgoing mock epic but something else.[14] Yet I believe with Jack that there is some truth in Joseph Warton's views, expressed in 1782. Warton thought that the original three-book poem was 'clear, consistent and of a piece':

> But in the year 1742, our poet was persuaded, unhappily enough, to add a *fourth* book to his *finished* piece, of such a very different cast and colour, as to render it at last [a] most motley composition... For one great purpose of this *fourth* book, (where, by the way, the hero does nothing at all) was to satirize and proscribe infidels, and free-thinkers, to leave the ludicrous for the serious, Grub-street for theology, the mock-heroic for metaphysics; which occasioned a marvellous mixture and jumble of images and sentiments, Pantomime and Philosophy, Journals and Moral evidence, Fleetditch and the High Priori road, *Curl* and *Clarke*.[15]

This is forcible and not without perception. I think we have to start by admitting that the epic fable does slow almost to a complete halt in Book IV, that the strong presence of London in the earlier books is largely dispersed, and that there is a marked shift in tone.

What then is the relation of the fourth book to the main

story line? An influential essay by George Sherburn proposes the idea that the comedies written by Henry Fielding during the 1730s supplied Pope with the image of a 'levée', with subjects crowding round a spurious queen and claiming rewards.[16] It has also been seen as a parody of Oxford degree ceremonies. Both of these interpretations have the incidental merit of linking the new scenario with Pope's description of the candidates for fame in *The Temple of Fame,* a poem which in a number of ways seem to offer antithetical sidelights on *The Dunciad.* Nevertheless, they hardly dispose of the problem. Sherburn's reading makes a virtue of the 'episodic' presentation in Book IV – it is all one with Fielding's technique, he tells us. Yet this does lend a bitty impression to the writing after the sweeping vision of Book III. Moreover, as we have seen, in the original version the prophecy uttered by Settle's ghost issued directly into the concluding lines on the triumph of Dulness. There is a case (to put it at its lowest) for asserting that this impressive setpiece comes best from a character in the story, one who is a seer and outside mortal experience, rather than from any godlike narrator standing beyond the action:

> Lo! the great Anarch's ancient reign restor'd,
> Light dies before her uncreating word:
> As one by one, at dread Medaea's strain,
> The sick'ning Stars fade off th'aethereal plain:
> As Argus' eyes, by Hermes' wand opprest,
> Clos'd one by one to everlasting rest;
> Thus at her felt approach, and secret might,
> Art after Art goes out, and all is Night.
>
> (A, III, 339–46)

The mention of a former empire is appropriate to the outgoing City Poet, the magical associations are appropriate to a vatic 'Sage', and the dissolution of the arts is well chronicled by a dead dramatist. It is a natural climax to the melodrama of Book III – a staggering intensification when it occurs in the discursive fourth book.

In my opinion it is best to admit that the *Greater Dunciad* pays for its increased range and resonance with some loss of structural coherence. It is all very well to say with John E. Sitter that 'there is little that can be called action in the conventional sense' in the poem, merely 'an abundance of activity'. But it does not follow that 'anything larger or more unified' has to be 'abstracted' from this activity.[17] Rather, the muddled and futile busyness that we observe in the final book confirms the truth already laid out in the main plot – that Dulness is terrifyingly positive despite her torpor, 'obliquely wadling to the mark in view' (1,172). For all her apparent sloth, she is far from purposeless: she has the energy of a slow but profound momentum – as Bentley is made to observe of the line 'Laborious, heavy, busy, bold, and blind' (I, 15):

> [Dulness] ·includes (as we see by the Poet's own words) Labour, Industry, and some degree of Activity and Boldness: a ruling principle not inert, but turning topsy-turvy the Understanding, and inducing an Anarchy or confused State of Mind.

The difference between sluggishness and total inertia is crucial to the poem. The first three books gives us an epic (at ordinary pace) of the deeply dull, whilst Book IV makes the plot stand still as Dulness gathers her forces. There *is* a cessation in the action, despite what some commentators have said; but this is part of the narrative of restoring native anarchy:

> But all the story of the night told over,
> And all their minds transfigur'd so together.
> More witnesseth than fancy's images,
> And grows to something of great constancy,
> But, howsoever, strange and admirable.

Borrowing Hippolyta's words from *A Midsummer Night's Dream* (V, i, 23–7), we might say that the story of eternal night shows us England as a whole (not just the dull) transfigured by the goddess in multiple ways, often rendered in the most fanciful images, and yet there is a fearful 'constancy' about it all. As Sitter remarks, '*The Dunciad* is an urban fairy tale, a Grub Street dream vision that assumes the proportions of a nightmare.'[18] Up to Book III the waking vision has some degree of connection; in the final book we have only the jagged non sequiturs of a dream.

The second problem concerns the substitution of a new laureate, Colley Cibber, in place of Lewis Theobald, who had occupied that position with every sign of adequacy in the first version. According to Warburton, Pope felt the need of 'a more considerable Hero', and was fortunately provided with Cibber, who suddenly launched into an assault upon Pope in 1742 after years of quietly enduring the worst that could be thrown at him. Of course Cibber had not been Poet Laureate when *The Dunciad* first appeared: he was appointed in 1730. It is just possible that Pope imagined Theobald might be the heir apparent, which would have confirmed his suitability for the role. But when Cibber got the job, a new set of circumstances presented themselves. The main fact was that Theobald had come well out of his dispute with Pope over the text of Shakespeare. When first cast as King Dunce, his reputation in this field had rested on *Shakespeare Restored* (1726). But in 1734 he brought out an edition of Shakespeare which comfortably outdid Pope's in the general opinion. It would therefore be tactless to go on needling Theobald for indifferent attainments as a scholar. If Pope was to leave him in possession of the part, he had to shift attention from Theobald the pedant to Theobald the hack dramatist. Most inconsiderately, Theobald showed less and less inclination to develop this side of his career. So Pope, boldly and wisely, opted for another tactic. He suppressed Theobald's part in the affair entirely – maybe an ironic comment on the transitory nature of duncely fame? And he put in a brand new hero, Cibber, in 1743.

The artistic effects of this change are many. Whatever his faults, Cibber was no pedant; and so one important strand in the poem underwent increased strain. *The Dunciad* being the sort of poem it was, Pope could not eliminate all reference to pedantry. So he transferred to Cibber, rather implausibly, the 'Gothic Library' (I, 145) once owned by Theobald. Despite some cunning attempts to paper over the cracks, e.g. by stressing 'patched-up plays' (Cibber was a great dramatic cobbler), the effort shows. Thus the line referring to 'hapless Shakespear, yet of Tibbald sore' (I, 133) is turned against Cibber in the note: 'It is not to be doubted by Bays [Cibber] was a subscriber to Tibbald's Shakespear'. Well, he was, but so were better and

worse men. Still less comforting was the knowledge that Cibber
had also subscribed to Pope's own Homer – a fact with which
the note wrestles a little uneasily. Apart from all this, there
was the consideration that Theobald had, unlike Cibber, collaborated with Settle, and had been personally responsible for
many harlequinades. Finally, it has been widely felt that the
egregious, bouncing Cibber could never be a proper representative of the dull. I don't think it avails much to say that Pope
meant a good deal more by his word 'dulness' than our present-
day sense of tedium. It would have been better for the dramatic
workings if Cibber had been more wooden, humourless and
thick-skinned than he really was. As it happened, the worst
you could call him was a lively dunce.[19]

Nevertheless, the advantages outweighed any loss of propriety. To start with, Cibber was known to a far wider public.
He had been prominent longer, and in fact was seventeen years
older than Theobald. As an actor he had specialized in the role
of fops, and this together with his self-display in the *Apology
for the Life of Mr Colley Cibber* (1740) laid him open to the charge
of coxcombry. 'Never had Impudence and Vanity so faithful
a Proffessor', wrote Pope of the *Apology* (*Corr,* iv, 438). Cibber
was above all the 'comedian', and this fitted him for the peacock
role which the poem bestows on him:

> The proud Parnassian sneer,
> The conscious simper, and the jealous leer,
> Mix on his look: All eyes direct their rays
> On him, and crowds turn Coxcombs as they gaze.
> His Peers shine round him with reflected grace,
> New edge their dulness, and new bronze their face.
>
> (II, 5–10)

Accustomed to facing the gaze of the public, Cibber gained
new eminence – of a sort – with his accession to the post of
Poet Laureate. *The Dunciad* is full of cruel jibes at Cibber's
lamentable performances in sustaining the level of mediocrity
which recent laureates had set. Further, Cibber was a theatrical
manager, who had presided over Drury Lane at the time when
tasteless spectacle filled the stage. As the ghost of Settle proclaims,

> See, see our own true Phoebus wears the bays!
> Our Midas sits Lord Chancellor of Plays!
>
> (III, 323–4)

Unlike Theobald, Cibber was a great organization man, with influence in the right places. He therefore makes a more sinister leader of the dunces, though a more patently absurd figure:

> Thou Cibber! thou, his Laurel shalt support,
> Folly, my son, has still a Friend at Court.
>
> (I, 299–300)

Cibber's very prominence in the culture meant that he served better than Theobald to express the spread and glamour of Dulness:

> In each she marks her Image full exprest,
> But chief in BAY's monster-breeding breast;
> Bays, form'd by nature Stage and Town to bless,
> And act, and be, a Coxcomb with success.
>
> (I, 107–10)

The arch-dunce, then, has put on theatrical representations of folly; but his own identity is just as absurd. That had never been true of Theobald, so the revised poem gets an additional charge of satiric energy.

The issue which has recently set off a great deal of debate is the attitude of Pope towards the dunces. According to John A. Jones, 'More than any other of Pope's satires, the *Dunciad* expresses towards its victims a serene and almost lyrical contempt'.[20] A namesake of that critic, Emrys Jones, contends that 'one seems to see *past* the personal names and topical allusions to a large fantasy world, an imaginative realm which is infused with a powerful sense of gratification and indulgence'. Further, the dunces are 'like unabashed small children', evoked in 'soft and delicate' poetry. The games they play give us 'a version of pre-literate infancy, and to enter [their world] is to experience a primitive sense of liberation'.[21] Not very remote are the views expressed in Howard Erskine-Hill's essay, already cited, which emphasizes the fascination of Pope for the monstrous images he has created. According to this reading, Pope chooses (or

is compelled by his artistic instincts) to *explore* Dulness, rather
than just satirize it.[22]

All these accounts have some cogency, and Emrys Jones
makes some particularly brilliant observations about the workings of the poem. But I think they can be carried too far. It
is easy to forget the element of retribution in *The Dunciad* – to
evade the fact that the dramatic climax is brought on by a vast
yawn, and hence to play down unduly the volume and intensity
of sheer contempt. Some of the grandest effects proceed from
something most unlike the 'double response' about which Dr
Erskine-Hill writes, and writes very eloquently; they derive from
a harshly unrelenting attitude and a masterful technique of be-
littlement. They recall not Spenser but Dryden:

> 'O born in sin, and forth in folly brought!
> Works damn'd, or to be damn'd! (your father's fault)
> Go, purify'd by flames ascend the sky,
> My better and more christian progeny!
> Unstain'd, untouch'd, and yet in maiden sheets;
> While all your smutty sisters walk the streets.
> Ye shall not beg, like gratis-giving Bland,
> Sent with a Pass, and vagrant thro' the land;
> Not sail, with Ward, to Ape-and-monkey climes,
> Where vile Mundungus trucks for viler rhymes;
> Nor sulphur-tipt, emblaze an Ale-house fire;
> Not wrap up Oranges, to pelt your sire!
> O! pass more innocent, in infant state,
> To the mild Limbo of our Father Tate:
> Or peaceably forgot, at once be blest
> In Shadwell's bosom with eternal Rest!
> Soon to that mass of Nonsense to return,
> Where things destroy'd are swept to things unborn.'
>   (I, 225–42)

This is Cibber addressing his works prior to burning them. We
could adduce it in support of Emrys Jones, for there is innocence, infancy, softness. Yet this apparent tenderness is cut
across by a deeper loathing: the ultimate fate of these books
is to return to premordial waste, 'swept' like garbage, and
lumped in with aborted foetuses. The language in which Pope

alludes to Cibber's children escapes libel only because it is too strong seemingly to apply ('smutty sisters'). Again and again the squalid destruction brings us back to the rawest sides of everyday living – *walk the streets, beg, vagrant, Ape-and-monkey, Alehouse fire, wrap up Oranges*. We are close to the outburst of Curll over *his* books in *A Further Account*:

> Are you not the beggarly Brood of fumbling *Journey-men*; born in *Garrets,* among *Lice* and *Cobwebs,* nurs'd upon *Grey Peas, Bullocks Liver,* and *Porter's Ale*? – Was not the first Light you saw, the *Farthing* Candle I paid for? Did you not come before your Time into *dirty Sheets* of brown Paper? ...Damn ye all, ye *Wolves* in *Sheeps Cloathing*; *Rags ye were, and to Rags ye shall return.*
>
> (*Prose*, I, 284)

In both cases Pope associates the products of the dull with dirt, disease, poverty, ugliness, unnatural birth and ultimate destruction. We cannot seriously look for 'ambiguity' in this genre scene. It is the 'mildness' that is illusory. Finally all Dulness relapses into the same sticky mess; and the agency of this process is a poetry instilled with ferocity and hatred:

> Mummius o'erhears him; Mummius, Fool-renown'd,
> Who like his Cheops stinks above the ground,
> Fierce as a startled Adder, swell'd, and said,
> Rattling an ancient Sistrum at his head.
>
> (IV, 371–4)

It is a modern sentimentality to assume that you can only see an object clearly if you bring 'compassion' to it. Pope let the dunces cavort in fantastic self-indulgence: but he did not come to love them on that account.

* * * * *

I have kept until last the most remarkable aspect of *The Dunciad* – its poetry. We come to the work nowadays caring little about Hanoverian politics, oblivious of Grub Street quarrels, profoundly undisturbed by the cultural malaise of the early eighteenth century. We know next to nothing concerning the principal actors in the story; as for the minor characters, we

are not altogether convinced that they existed on the face of
the earth. Yet the poem lives, abundantly, powerfully, creatively.
This is above all an effect of the writing, for there are few books
which make such extraordinary use of the resources of the
English language. The dynamic range of the verse extends from
a gentle misapplied lyricism to a coruscating wit. The invention
is endless. Books and writers are constantly becoming *things,*
with their own malevolent will:

> Thro' Lud's fam'd gates, along the well-known Fleet
> Rolls the black troop, and overshades the street,
> 'Till show'rs of Sermons, Characters, Essays,
> In circling fleeces whiten all the ways:
> So clouds replenish'd from some bog below,
> Mount in dark volumes, and descend in snow.
>
> (II, 359–64)

We switch with bewildering speed from the mythical to the
actual, and the distant to the immediate:

> Millions and millions on those banks he views,
> Thick as the stars of night, or morning dews,
> As thick as bees o'er vernal blossoms fly,
> As thick as eggs at Ward in Pillory.
>
> (III, 31–4)

Abstract and concrete blend ('Sooterkins of Wit') in a metaphysical embrace:

> Round him much Embryo, much Abortion lay,
> Much future Ode, and abdicated Play;
> Nonsense precipitate, like running Lead,
> That slip'd thro' Cracks and Zig-zags of the Head;
> All that on Folly Frenzy could beget,
> Fruits of dull Heat, and Sooterkins of Wit.
> Next, o'er his Books his eyes began to roll,
> In pleasing memory of all he stole,
> How here he snipp'd, how there he plunder'd snug
> And suck'd all o'er, like an industrious Bug.
> Here lay poor Fletcher's half-eat scenes, and here
> The Frippery of crucify'd Moliere;

Wish'd he had blotted for himself before.
There hapless Shakespeare, yet of Tibbald sore,
                              (I, 121–34)

A number of recurrent images are scattered through the text.
The idea of miscegenation or mixed marriage is one: this is
encapsulated in a single couplet,

Norton, from Daniel and Ostroea sprung,
Bless'd with his father's front, and mother's tongue.
                              (II, 415–16)

'Daniel' is the real Daniel Defoe; 'Ostroea' the mythical name
of an oyster wench, allegedly a street seller with whom Defoe
had taken up.[23] Another common notion is that of disease:
Dulness is presented as a biological micro-organism. A third
example is the surreal landscape of a world shaken by some
great calamity of nature. A fourth is the evocation of insanity,
brought up at the start by the Bedlam setting. All four of these
crop up in a superb passage in the opening book:

Here she beholds the Chaos dark and deep,
Where nameless Somethings in their causes sleep,
'Till genial Jacob, or a warm Third day,
Call forth each mass, a Poem or a Play:
How hints, like spawn, scarce quick in embryo lie,
How new-born nonsense first is taught to cry,
Maggots half-form'd in rhyme exactly meet,
And learn to crawl upon poetic feet.
Here one poor word an hundred clenches makes,
And ductile dulness new meanders takes;   64
There motley Images her fancy strike,
Figures ill pair'd, and Similes unlike.
She sees a Mob of Metaphors advance,
Pleas'd with the madness of the mazy dance:
How Tragedy and Comedy embrace;   69
How Farce and Epic get a jumbled race;
How time himself stands still at her command,
Realms shift their place, and Ocean turns to land.
Here gay Description Aegypt glads with show'rs,
Or gives to Zembla fruits, to Barca flow'rs;

> Glitt'ring with ice here hoary hills are seen,
> There painted vallies of eternal green,
> In cold December fragrant chaplets blow,
> And heavy harvests nod beneath the snow.
>
> (I, 55–78)

The rendition only acquires that hideous strength because the picture of formlessness is so formally organized. Dulness contradicts everything Pope's art stands for. As a result, the orderly presentation throws into relief the messiness which is being presented. All Pope's accumulated skills help this effect: the surge of the verse, the sharply defined couplets, the decisive rhymes, the unfailing clarity. Set against this we have a series of vacillations and muddles – note the repeated *or* constructions, representing the arbitrary choices of non-art. Everything *within* the picture is *dark, deep, in embryo, half-form'd, ductile, motley, ill pair'd, mazy, jumbled.* The constituent parts are *nameless somethings* (Pope's style is inalienably precise); other nouns suggest the same quality – *mass, spawn, nonsense, mob, madness.* For the Augustans, the primal fear was not that things would fall apart, but that everything would somehow merge. Hence the terror that lurks behind the comedy.[24]

Now it is true that the participants seem to be enjoying themselves, and so is Dulness as she contemplates them. But these races and dances are more like the activities of bacteria than civilized social diversions. *Embrace* (line 69) has obscene overtones. The *meanders* (line 64) are not harmless wanderings but betray the random operations of ignorance. Pope lets us see the manic energy, but the logic of his own style condemns the muddle. Similarly at the later juncture:

> Thence a new world to Nature's laws unknown,
> Breaks out refulgent, with a heav'n its own:
> Another Cynthia her new journey runs,
> And other planets circle other suns.
> The forests dance, the rivers upward rise,
> Whales sport in woods, and dolphins in the skies;
> And last, to give the whole creation grace,
> Lo! one vast Egg produces human race.
>
> (III, 241–8)

Erskine-Hill is right to say that Pope 'is clearly fascinated by
the surrealistic strangeness of it all.'[25] But again the syntax
points up the arbitrary element; the effect of the antithesis in
line 246 is to make us feel, 'If whales can be found in woods,
well why not dolphins in the sky?' In other words, the symmetry
of the phrasing underlines the perversity of this 'new world':
the tidiness of the language ('last . . .') brings out its monstrosity.

A great deal of the poem works on a less cosmic plane. There
is for instance, some audacious punning:

> Where Bentley late tempestuous wont to sport
> In troubled waters, but now sleeps in Port.
>
> (IV, 201–2)

Or this, using the name of fearsome Judge Page:

> Morality…
> Gasps, when they straiten at each end the cord,
> And dies, when Dulness gives her Page the word.
>
> (IV, 29–30)

There is ingenious wordplay with other duncely names:

> And lo! her bird, (a monster of a fowl,)
> Something betwixt a Heideggre and owl).
>
> (I, 289–90)

More subtly, the lines on the aged critic Oldmixon as he muses
on the passage of time begin thus:

> In naked majesty Oldmixon stands…
>
> (II, 283)

The iambic rhythm impels us to reverse the normal stress (*Old*-
mixon) and place the accent on the second syllable: Old *Mix*on–
that is, ancient dunghill. *The Dunciad* is always taking huge
linguistic risks.

It is difficult to summarize in a few words the varied capacities
of the poetry – its power of comic exposure is matched by its
haunting evocative strain, as in the beautifully mannered word
picture of the Grand Tour (IV, 292–336). One can only pick
a final instance, the passage which follows the yawn of Dulness.

At this climactic moment, Pope's talent for striking the right level of tone did not fail him:

> More she had spoke, but yawn'd – All Nature nods:
> What Mortal can resist the Yawn of Gods?
> Churches and Chapels instantly it reach'd;
> (St. James's first, for leaden Gilbert preach'd)
> Then catch'd the Schools; the Hall scarce kept awake;
> The Convocation gap'd, but could not speak:
> Lost was the Nation's Sense, nor could be found,
> While the long solemn Unison went round:
> Wide, and more wide, it spread o'er all the realm;
> Ev'n Palinurus nodded at the Helm:
> The Vapour mild o'er each Committee crept;
> Unfinish'd Treaties in each Office slept;
> And Chiefless Armies doz'd out the Campaign;
> And Navies yawn'd for Orders on the Main.
>
> (IV, 605–18)

A mounting intensity suffuses the writing. With the long un-broken clause, 'While the long solemn Unison went round', we are made aware of a kind of droning conformity. The conclud-ing lines are conceived with ironic amplitude, as though ac-knowledging that it is an achievement to create such universal somnolence. This illustrates the fact that Pope needed to be a major poet to do justice to the triumph of Dulness. No Smith-field bard, prompt in delivering panegyrics on *Augusta Trium-phans,* could have made us believe in the restoration of an empire. A slender talent would have been overborne by the heroic and prophetic obligations of the undertaking. Yet it was also necessary that a central *comic* vision should inform the poem, for the day of straight epic was done. In Pope the hour found its man, for he was learned enough not to misapply his learning, serious enough not to solemnize a farce, artistic enough not to fear stretching the confines of art.

CHAPTER NINE

A poet's prose

It comes as a surprise that Pope should have troubled to write prose at all. A man capable of producing anything from a metaphysical treatise to a casual dinner invitation in the most polished verse seems scarcely to have any need for the other medium. Yet in fact Pope did put together a considerable body of work in prose. At the head of his achievement here lie his letters, among the most important to appear in a century when correspondence counted for a great deal. There are also some interesting critical pronouncements, the varied range of Scriblerian and satiric offerings, and a small contribution to drama. Little account is generally taken of this side of Pope's career. It deserves closer attention, and offers ample rewards in enjoyment and literary distinction.

The earliest work to be published and acknowledged by Pope embodies a number of journalistic papers. When Pope was first coming to notice, the genre of the hour was the essay. Addison and Steele had struck an immensely popular chord with the *Tatler* (1709–11) and *Spectator* (1711–12). Swift in the *Examiner* and Defoe in the *Review,* for that matter, had enlisted the periodical press for their own political and economic ends. But it was the more relaxed moral essay practised above all by Addison that offered Pope an opportunity. In later years the relations of Pope and Addison were to be clouded by 'the curse of party' and various rivalries. But Addison was a significant example to the younger man at the start of his career. Pope is known to have contributed two or three papers to the *Spectator,* and Norman Ault assigned another half dozen to him.[1] None is very important or distinctive, though the mock proposals for a new kind of newspaper in Nos. 452 and 457 (*Prose,* 56–62) are diverting enough. After the demise of the *Spectator* Steele brought out a successor called the *Guardian,* and here Pope took a more prominent part. He wrote an amusing dissertation on the obsequious dedications then in vogue (No. 4). There is a famous essay on gardening (No. 173), recommending a more natural style of landscape design, and a witty Addisonian sketch of a 'club of little men' (Nos. 91–2), with Pope himself as 'Dick Distick' – 'He is a lively little Creature, with long Arms and Legs: A Spider is no ill Emblem of him. He hath been taken at a Distance for a *small Windmill*' (*Prose,* 124). The best of these papers, however, is the celebrated essay on pastorals (No. 40), a cruel but hilarious demolition of a rival, Ambrose Philips, ironically criticizing Pope's own pastorals for being too much like Virgil.

After this time Pope rarely strayed into journalism, although he contributed to some imponderable extent to the *Grub-street Journal* in the 1730s. The middle years of his career saw the publication of a number of critical essays, mentioned in earlier chapters, attached to one or other of his own works. The 1717 collected works contained a preface and the discourse on pastoral; the *Iliad* had its preface (1715) and the *Odyssey* its post-script (1725). This last year saw the appearance of the preface to Shakespeare as well. By far the most distinguished of these, and the most revelatory for the workings of Pope's creative mind, was the essay at the head of the *Iliad,* together with many important notes to the text.

Meanwhile, Pope had turned to a new mode of expression, the satirical pamphlet. His first shot, *The Critical Specimen* (1711), was only partially successful; its promise of a life of 'the renown'd Rinaldo Furioso', alias John Dennis, raises more comic possibilities than it is able to sustain. But Pope homed right on to the target with *The Narrative of Dr Robert Norris* (1713), in which Dennis is shown as a raving lunatic attended by the quack 'mad-doctor' Norris. As in most of these pamphlets, there is a strong present-tense feel to the writing; the references are closely particularized, and one thinks of Pope's later poetry (say, the *Imitations of Horace*) rather than the verse collected in 1717:

> ...Secondly, he hath given out about *Fleetstreet* and the *Temple,* that I was an Accomplice with his Bookseller, who visited him with Intent to take away drivers valuable Manuscripts, without paying him Copy-Money.

Thirdly, he hath told others, that I am no graduate Physician, and that he hath seen me upon a Mountebank Stage in *Moorfields,* when he had Lodgings in the College there.

Fourthly, Knowing that I had much Practice in the City, he reported at the *Royal Exchange, Custom-house,* and other Places adjacent, that I was a foreign Spy, employ'd by the *French* King to convey him into *France...*

(*Prose,* 167–8)

This manner is developed and refined, if that is not too soft a word, in three pamphlets directed against the rascally publisher Edmund Curll. The first two date from 1716, and show Pope at his most brutal best:

For Mr. *Manwaring*'s *Life,* I ask Mrs. *Old—d*'s Pardon: Neither *His,* nor my Lord *Halifax*'s Lives, though they were of great Service to their Country, were of any to me: But I was resolved, since I could not print their Works while they liv'd, to print their Lives after they were dead.

(*Prose,* 264–5)

Curll had brought out instant, and altogether unauthorized, biographies of Lord Halifax and Arthur Maynwaring (whose mistress was the famous actress Anne Oldfield). The barb could scarcely be sharper. Pope brought out a sequel around 1720, but it is less effective. There is, too, the first of many thrusts at Colley Cibber in *A Clue to the Non-Juror* (1718).

By this time Pope was already an experienced writer in the Scriblerian way. The celebrated Scriblerus Club grew up around 1713, with a membership consisting of Pope, Swift, John Gay, Dr Arbuthnot and Thomas Parnell: the chief minister, Robert Harley, was allowed a sort of honorific attachment.[2] The plan was to produce a series of *Works of the Unlearned* (*Prose,* 62: *Corr,* i, 195) in which fashionable pedantries should be parodied. There is something a little cliquish and Frenchified about this group production, and for a long time the output of the club was generally disregarded. However, the enterprise is now rightly looked on more respectfully. Not only did it spawn two important full-dress works, *Peri Bathous* and *The Memoirs of*

---

the College i.e. Bedlam

Martinus Scriblerus, it also contributed a good deal to master-pieces such as *Gulliver's Travels* and *The Dunciad* – in mood and method, and perhaps too in detailed content.

Moreover, the shorter squibs emanating from the club include some lively and amusing items. *A Key to the Lock* (1715) is prob-ably the unaided work of Pope, but it is utterly Scriblerian in its solemn reading of *The Rape of the Lock* as a treasonable mes-sage enciphered in the poetry. *Annus Mirabilis* (1722) is a splendid hoax report of a universal sex change; Pope and Arbuthnot (the likely authors) joyfully exploit the bawdy potential of this event. And there are vestiges of Scriblerian drama. Pope *may* have contributed something to Gay's one act 'tragi-comi-pas-toral farce' *The What d'ye Call it* (1715), though this is a matter of doubt. He almost certainly had a hand in a spin-off pamphlet offering 'a complete key' to the farce. The play itself is a frolic-some romp, though it cries out for music such as Thomas Arne later gave to comic operas of the mid century. The poet Cowper, who was far from loving all things Augustan, later remarked that 'the most celebrated association of clever fellows this country ever saw did not think it beneath them to unite their strength and abilities in the composition of a song' for this play.[3] Colla-boration is seldom given this amount of credit. More substantial is the full-length farce *Three Hours After Marriage* (1717) by Pope, Gay and Arbuthnot. This is excellent stage comedy as well as amusing social criticism. It centres round a credulous Scri-blerus-type figure called Dr Fossile, representing an able but vainglorious pioneer of geology called John Woodward. Around this doting pedant play a variety of characters including a pretentious lady dramatist, a scheming theatrical producer (representing Cibber, and amazingly *played by him*), and a foolish Longinian critic – John Dennis yet again. The action is pure Feydeau, until the introduction of a mummy and a crocodile in the last act suggest surrealist theatre of the twentieth century. But – unlike Dada, say – Scriblerian satire avoids the anarchic. Throughout the sexual intrigue and personal caricature there runs a strong vein of common sense, insight and humanity. Absurd behaviour is shown to proceed from vanity, prejudice, blindness – not just the situations but the *ideas* are silly.

The two major works of Scriblerus proper came out some

years later. Pope put out *Peri Bathous: or, The Art of Sinking in Poetry* in a volume of miscellanies in March 1728, maybe as a preparatory step towards *The Dunciad*. It is an ironic manual of rhetoric, compiled by the arch-pedant Scriblerus, and designed to do for the literary depths what the classical treatise *Peri Hupsous* had done for the heights.[4] Longinus and the Sublime were then on everyone's lips, and Pope had an easy target. In addition, it is a new *ars poetica,* performing the service for the present which Horace had undertaken in the past. It is thus one more blow in the Ancients and Moderns controversy – a debate one can never escape in this period. Finally, it is a wickedly accurate survey of contemporary writing, allowing Pope to unload scores of examples of bad poetry which he had treasured up for years. A number of old accounts are settled, and a few new enmities carefully contracted with a view to replies and duncely potentialities.

There are sixteen chapters, twelve of them relating directly to Longinus, followed by four 'loose' sections. The underlying human compulsion towards the 'profound' – that is, involuntary anticlimax – is described, together with its physical concomitants:

Is there not an Architecture of Vaults and Cellars, as well as of lofty Domes and Pyramids? Is there not as much Skill and Labour in making of *Dykes,* as in raising of *Mounts?* Is there not an Art of *Diving* as well as of *Flying?* And will any sober Practitioner affirm, That a diving Engine is not of singular Use in making him long-winded, assisting his Sight, and furnishing him with other ingenious means of keeping under Water?

(*PB,* 15)

We are told of how a 'true genius' in the profound operates – 'His Design ought to be like a Labyrinth, out of which nobody can get you clear but himself' (18). The need for monstrosity is stressed:

Nothing seem'd more plain to our great Authors, than that the World had long been weary of natural Things. How much the contrary is form'd to please, is evident from the universal

Applause daily given, to the admirable Entertainments of *Harlequins* and *Magicians* on the Stage. When an Audience behold a Coach turn'd into a Wheel-barrow, a Conjurer into an Old Woman, or a Man's Head where his Heels should be; how are they struck with Transport and Delight? ... He ought therefore to render himself Master of this happy and antinatural way of thinking to such a degree, as to be able, on the appearance of any Object, to furnish his Imagination with Ideas infinitely below it. And his Eyes should be like unto the wrong end of a Perspective Glass, by which all the Objects of Nature are lessen'd.

(19)

This recalls the attack on popular culture we saw in *The Dunciad,* but it is also a thoroughgoing anti-poetic. The Augustans believed that poetry should not disperse grandeur by comparing great with little – witness Johnson's criticism of the metaphysical poets. The art of sinking, it will prove, lies in consistently flouting this rule and others like it. Degrading and inappropriate similes are cited from a wide range of sources to illustrate how the true voice of bathos sounds in poetry.

So the onslaught continues, with apt illustrations at every turn – and here and there an invented example, where none was readily to hand. In the sixth chapter Pope shifts to a more particularized mode of satire. He supplies a bestiary of contemporary poets – each writer listed by his initials, and identified with a given species. These strange creatures have some of the threatening, amorphous, subhuman quality of the dunces:

...5.   The *Didappers* are Authors that keep themselves long *out* of sight, under water, and *come up* now and then when you *least expected* them. *L.W.* – *D.* Esq; The Hon. Sir *W.Y.*

...6.   The *Porpoises* are unweildy and big; they put all their Numbers into a great *Turmoil* and *Tempest,* but whenever they appear in *plain Light,* (which is seldom) they are only *shapeless* and *ugly Monsters. I.D. C.G. I.O.*

(27)

It does not matter whom these initials represent: they are sufficiently identified by their unlovely antics and submarine haunts.

Pope displays no bitterness – on the contrary, he seems to take an intense delight in the imaginative play and zoological invention required of him.

After anatomizing some of the favourite rhetorical turns of the profound poets – roundabout language, highfalutin' jargon, and the rest – Pope devotes a special section (Chapters X–XI) to the perversions of metaphor which they favour, ending up with 'the Inanity, or Nothingness', and similar figures. Chapter XII, 'Of Expression', sets out the prevailing styles of the day, whether 'florid', 'pert', 'alamode', 'finical' or 'cumbrous'. Each of these is differentiated with some care, with apt illustrations to drive home the point. Then come the four chapters with no Longinian basis. They cover a Swiftian 'project for the advancement of the bathos', requiring the sponsorship of church and state for a three-story computer bank which 'composers' will be taught to manipulate like an organ keyboard. Another characteristic Augustan concern, how to make panegyrics and satires (especially when dedicating) is discussed next. There is a recipe for writing epics, drawn from a paper originally published in the *Guardian*. Finally, a little irrelevant perhaps but marvellous fun, another project: this time a public theatrical academy, just the sort of thing the author of *A Tale of a Tub* would like, with all sorts of imposing duties set aside for it. As so often, the institution is to take over existing quarters in London:

> If *Westminster Hall* be not allotted to this Service, (which by reason of its Proximity to the two Chambers of Parliament above mention'd, seems not altogether improper;) it is left to the Wisdom of the Nation whether *Somerset House* may not be demolish'd, and a *Theatre* built upon that Scite, which lies convenient to receive Spectators from the County of *Surrey,* who may be wafted thither by Water-Carriage, esteem'd by all Projectors the cheapest whatsoever.
>
> (88)

And of course the theatre should be 'environ'd with a fair Quadrangle of Buildings, fitted for the Accommodation of decay'd *Criticks* and *Poets,'* headed by the laureate. No satire by Pope or Swift is complete without some mock philanthropy on behalf of superannuated wits.

The other principal outcome of the club's project were *The Memoirs of Martinus Scriblerus,* finally published by Pope amongst his collected prose in 1741. It is a collaborative work, probably written at intervals between 1714 and 1727. Though rich and complex in ideas, it is too jumbled in arrangement to have attained widespread popularity. Yet it is one of the most important precursors of *Tristram Shandy,* and an illuminating analogue to Swift's *Tale* and Pope's *Dunciad.* It traces the life history of the blockhead scholar, from the portents which surrounded his birth up to his planned departure on his travels in 1699. From the text, it appears that these were in fact identical with Gulliver's! The book is too episodic for its own comfort, but at its best it is one of the funniest satires on intellectual matters which has come down to us – Cervantes, Rabelais and Erasmus are among its presiding spirits. Martin's education is especially well handled, in terms recalling *Peri Bathous,* and there are some brilliant cameos – Martin's mechanistic practice in medicine (Chapter X), the story of a young man who becomes passionate and erotically infatuated with himself; and the notorious interlude of 'the double mistress' (Chapter XIV–XV). This portion was generally omitted from the text until 1950, and still is less well known than it should be. The story is based on a pair of real-life Siamese twins who toured Europe as a spectacle in the early part of the century. The hands of Pope and Arbuthnot seem to be strongest here, with Pope contributing his usual vein of *risqué* allusion. Briefly, the Scriblerian twins are joined in the region of their genitals. However, they turn out to possess separate organs, which causes obvious embarrassment when each becomes sexually involved. Martin becomes enamoured of Lindamira, whilst her sister Indamora falls for Martin (the names are drawn from contemporary novelettes). In time Martin marries Lindamira, while a black prince named Ebn-Hai-Paw-Waw carries off Indamora (and of course Lindamira at the same time). Protracted legal squabbles follow, reported in solemn detail, and canon law is ransacked for precedents. The comic possibilities of this misapplied learning are wonderfully well exploited, and it is noteworthy that the sexual implications are soon drowned in a welter of logic, sophistry, pedantry and confused authorities. Ultimately the case goes to appeal, and both

marriages are dissolved. It is one of the finest setpieces in Augustan satire.

Soon afterwards we take leave of Martin, as I mentioned,
when he is about to embark on his travels. But not before we
learn of some great discoveries he has made, and are presented
with a list of works beginning with 'a complete Digest of the
Laws of Nature' (*MS*, 167). We are further told of his numerous
projects 'directed to the universal Benefit of Mankind'. He plans
to refute Newton's theory of gravity and place lighthouses at
each pole of the earth 'to supply the defect of Nature, and
to make the Longitude as easy to be calculated as the Latitude'
(168). But he is also adept in medical research, in the arts and
in politics. As for instance:

> In Architecture, he builds not with so much regard to present
> symmetry or conveniency, as with a Thought well worthy a
> true lover of Antiquity, to wit, the noble effect a Building
> shall have to posterity, when it shall fall and become a Ruin.
> (169)

We shall assuredly meet Martin again in the Grand Academy
of Lagado. All in all, there is much which recalls Swift in the
Memoirs. But if there was a single organizing spirit, *primus inter
pares,* then it was Pope; and he may reasonably be looked on
as the general editor. The *Memoirs* deserve a more prominent
place in any reckoning of his achievement than they habitually
get.

*   *   *   *   *

The same is true of Pope's correspondence. It covers forty years,
and traverses an immense range of moods and topics. In particular, the letters which survive from the 1730s make up by
far the most important part of Pope's later prose – otherwise
only a stray pamphlet or two remains from this decade. Not
often self-revelatory in any obvious sense, they nonetheless
present a marvellously rich picture of the poet's life and times.
In his earlier years his style tends to be consciously smart, sometimes even cute: there is a dangerous prevalence of whimsy
in places. Later on, the besetting sin is more commonly a portentous exhibition of disinterest – a noble contempt for the

world, with ill-disguised self-pity creeping in at the edges. But against this we can set hundreds of simple, moving and affectionate messages. There is wit, compassion, geniality, concern. The appearance of George Sherburn's superb edition in 1956, as a matter of fact, provoked a small crisis of conscience in English studies: even professed admirers had not realized just how seriously Pope took the obligations of friendship, how often he did good by stealth, or how patiently (for instance) he looked after his troublesome in-laws, the Dickensian brood of Racketts. As the full body of letters came to light, it was evident that Pope's concept of friendship – like his notion of filial respect – was a matter of practice as well as precept.

One finds Pope in a variety of roles in his correspondence, as in his poetry. This has led some to cast doubt on his 'sincerity'. Moreover, in this case romantic prejudice has a strong circumstantial case. To be blunt, Pope doctored his letters for publication, having carefully set up the position in which their appearance in print (then an indecorous use of private letters) could be accepted by the public. The full story is too long to tell here. It would be like trying to summarize the plot of a classic Hollywood gangster film. Nor is the comparison all that inapt: there were mysterious visitors, voices from the grave, double-bluffs and a whole imbroglio of deception. Even Sherburn, a sober writer, refers to 'melodramatic intrigues'.[5] Pope had chosen for himself, too, what we have learnt to call a 'fall guy'. This was the scandalous bookseller, Edmund Curll. Actually Curll was not wholly worsted; and even when put in the wrong, he minded very little. He did after all produce the first edition of some of the most notable letters in the language – by Swift and others, apart from Pope – and he had plenty of opportunities to issue his familiar threats and bluster in the press. Scandal must advertise; and anything which gave Curll a chance to flaunt his productions he welcomed with enthusiasm. For him no publicity was bad publicity. In the end, though neither Pope nor Curll emerges from the transaction with great credit, the correspondence which began to filter out in 1735 marked a considerable breakthrough in literary habits. A taboo had been destroyed, and henceforth personal letters would be eligible as *belles lettres*. Without this episode it is doubtful whether men

like Horace Walpole and Gray would have lavished so many
skills on their correspondence, so as to make it seem natural
and unaffected.

It might seem surprising, in the light of all this, that Pope's
own private epistles could ever be fresh in style or spirit. Yet
they regularly are, even those touched up for the press. This
arises mainly from the vivacity and imagination which went into
their making, well evoked by Maynard Mack.[6] Some of the most
common subjects are books, politics, health, gardening, travel
and morality. In general the literary criticism is disappointing,
but there are some helpful insights into Pope's own struggles
as a writer – e.g. his weariness with the protracted Homeric
undertaking. The successive stages in the genesis of *The Dunciad*
are also closely charted. As for the other topics, it is chiefly owing
to the letters that we can fit together something approaching
a close medical history of Pope, along with his attitudes towards
illness in others, whilst his growing mania for gardens (a topic
I will return to in the final chapter) is fully documented. For
some tastes there is too much sententious musing on the good
life, retirement and such matters; but contemporaries expected
it – and Pope took advantage of that to offer those more
searching reflections on life which his semi-outcast state had
prompted.

One of the major topics, however, has been surprisingly
neglected. It seems generally accepted that Pope 'is not
interested in places and happenings' and that 'the letters offer
no chronicle of events, no portfolio of scenes and views, no
real history, social or political, of his times'.[7] There are certainly
few setpieces commemorating grand national occasions, in the
way that Horace Walpole immortalized the funeral of George
II. But it would surely take an imperceptive reader to miss the
pressure of events such as the South Sea Bubble, the exile of
Atterbury or the various crises faced by the Opposition in the
1730s. And in my judgment the 'portfolio of scenes and views'
is as remarkable as that afforded by any writer in the language.
Year after year Pope logs his travels to country houses and to
Bath. His unfailing sense of the picturesque was already enlisted,
because one function of these annual 'rambles' was to find suitable subjects for his pencil. Beyond this, however, there is a

constant urge to animate scenes through the imagination. In the early letters, particularly where Pope is writing to a woman, the landscape is likely to be transformed into a vision, charged with ghostly historical presences. Later on, with more worldly and masculine correspondents to the fore, we usually get a less rhapsodic account. But there is still a splendid power, recalling Dickens, to imbue a locality with feeling and with haunting suggestion.

This descriptive skill could be illustrated at great length. It is found in a number of moonlight walks and rustic idylls (e.g. *Corr,* i, 330, 393). Often it goes with rueful nostalgia or playful fantasy (ii, 86); sometimes there is a prescient air of the gothick:

> I came from Stonor (its Master not being at home) to Oxford the same night. Nothing could have more of that Melancholy which once us'd to please me, than that days journey: For after having passd thro' my favorite Woods in the forest, with a thousand Reveries of past pleasures; I rid over hanging hills, whose tops were edgd with Groves, & whose feet water'd with winding rivers, listening to the falls of Cataracts below, & the murmuring of Winds above. The gloomy Verdure of Stonor succeeded to these, & then the Shades of the Evening overtook me, the Moon rose in the clearest Sky I ever saw, by whose solemn light I pac'd on slowly, without company, or any interruption to the range of my thoughts. About a mile before I reachd Oxford, all the Night bells toll'd, in different notes; the Clocks of every College answered one another; & told me, some in a deeper, some in a softer voice, that it was eleven a clock.
>
> All this was no ill preparation to the life I have led since; among those old walls, venerable Galleries, Stone Portico's, studious walks & solitary Scenes of the University. I wanted nothing but a black Gown and a Salary, to be as meer a Bookworm as any there. I conform'd myself to the College hours, was rolld up in books & wrapt in mediatation, lay in one of the most ancient, dusky parts of the University, and was as dead to the world as any Hermite of the desart.
>
> (i, 429–30)

This is a perfectly accurate description of a journey in its way, though it lacks the detail of a Dorothy Wordsworth. What distinguishes it, apart from the gentle humour, is a kind of mantic awareness, born of a strong sense of the past.

However, Pope's accounts can be much more robust, as the immediately preceding letter, to the same recipients (Martha and Teresa Blount) shows. The concrete immediacy of the language has a Falstaffian ring to it:

> For I met the Prince [of Wales] with all his Ladies (tho few or none of his Lords) on horseback coming from Hunting. Mrs Bellendine & Mrs Lepell took me into protection (contrary to the Laws against harbouring Papists), & gave me a Dinner, with something I liked better, an opportunity of conversation with Mrs Howard. We all agreed that the life of a Maid of Honor was of all things the most miserable; & wished that every Woman who envyd it had a Specimen of it. To eat Westphalia Ham in a morning, ride over Hedges & ditches on borrowed Hacks, come home in the heat of the day with a Feavor, & what is worse a hundred times, a red Mark in the forhead with a Beaver hatt; all this may qualify them to make excellent Wives for Fox-hunters, & bear abundance of ruddy-complexion'd Children. As soon as they can wipe off the Sweat of the day, they must simper an hour, & catch cold, in the Princesses apartment; from thence *To Dinner, with what appetite they may*—And after that, till midnight, walk, work, or think, which they please? I can easily believe, no lone House in Wales, with a Mountain & a Rookery, is more contemplative than this Court; and as a proof of it I need only tell you Mrs Lepell walk'd all alone with me three or 4 hours, by moonlight; and we mett no Creature of any quality, but the King, who gave audience all alone to the Vice-Chamberlen, under the Garden-wall.
>
> (i, 427)

This is not unlike Fanny Burney's complaints about the monotony of court life, only better tempered. Of course, the effects are carefully contrived; but mark the skill with which the cadences are arranged, so the final sentence comes with surprise on the king in an anticlimactic parenthesis.

Pope's eyes are always open. He is particularly fond of

autumn, the season then assigned to contemplative activities, and depicts the opportunities it offers in 'prospects' to the painter (ii, 330). But as well as this generalized atmospheric scenery, he can give us the complete guidebook when called on, as at Sherborne:

> You come first out of the house into a green Walk of Standard Lymes with a hedge behind them that makes a Colonnade, thence into a little triangular wilderness, from whose Centre you see the town of Sherborne in a valley, interspersd with trees. From the corner of this you issue at once upon a high green Terras the whole breadth of the Garden, which has five more green Terras's hanging under each other, without hedges, only a few pyramid yews & large round Honisuckles between them. The Honisuckles hereabouts are the largest & finest I ever saw. You'l be pleased when I tell you the Quarters of the above mentioned little Wilderness are filld with these & with Cherry trees of the best kinds all within reach of the hand. At the ends of these Terras's run two long Walks under the Side walls of the Garden which communicate with the other Terras's that front these opposite. Between, the Vally is layd level and divided into two regular Groves of Horse chestnuts, and a Bowling-green in the middle of about 180 foot. This is bounded behind with a Canall, that runs quite across the Groves & also along one Side, in the form of a T. Behind this, is a Semicircular Berceau, and a Thicket of mixd trees that compleats the Crown of the Amfitheatre which is of equal extent with the Bowling-green.

And so on, for several more sentences full of precise directions and dimensions ('When you are at the left corner of the Canal and the Chestnut groves in the bottom, you turn of a sudden under very old trees into the deepest Shade...') Imperceptibly an emotional grading seeps into the writing:

> You first see an old Tower penetrated by a large Arch, and others above it thro which the whole Country appears in prospect, even when you are at the top of the other ruins, for they stand very high, & the Ground slopes down on all sides. These venerable broken Walls, some Arches almost entire

of 30 or 40 ft deep, some open like Portico's with fragments of pillars, some circular or inclosed on three sides, but exposed at the top, with Steps which Time has made of disjointed Stones to climb to the highest parts of the Ruin....

(ii, 237–8)

Anyone who has ever tried to draw a scale map in words will know how hard it is to be simple, literal and interesting. This letter to Martha Blount (22 June 1724?) is a good example of Pope's finished attainments as a descriptive writer.

Many of the letters are irradiated by wit; almost all are leavened by humour and invention. Pope strikes a variety of poses: sometimes he is the humble supplicant, begging fair treatment for his Homer advertisement from the editor of the *London Gazette*: 'Also to stand at the head of the more vulgar advertisements at least rankd before Eloped wives, if not before Lost Spaniels & Strayd Geldings' (ii, 285). A few pages later we find him in biblical vein:

My Lord [Bathurst] – There was a Man in the Land of Twitnam, called Pope. He was a Servant of the Lord Bathurst of those days, a Patriarch of great Eminence, for getting children, at home & abroad. But his Care for his Family, and his Love for strange women, caused the said Lord to forget all his Friends of the Male-sex; insomuch that he knew not, nor once remembered, there was such a man in the Land of Twitnam as aforesaid. It were to be wisht, he would come & see; or if nothing else would move him, there are certain Handmaids belonging to the said Pope which are comely in their goings, yea which go comelily.... My dear Lord, adieu, (if Adieu be not too impertinent, pretending a word, where one has never once met)....

(ii, 292)

A rebuke for inattention could scarcely be more felicitiously transformed. Bathurst in fact occasioned many of Pope's best letters in his middle years, full of robust and insubordinate fun. There is also an early verse letter, printed by Curll and never disavowed by Pope (i, 25–9). Towards the end of Pope's life, though the tone is frequently more mordant, the play of his mind remains agile: many of the letters to Swift combine a keen sense of loss for that which time has erased with a joyous eye for absurdity. The sturdy Hugh Bethel always prompted lively and unfussy letters from his friend; whilst the eccentric retired general, Peterborough, inspired many delightful messages, including one in which Pope poses as his abandoned wife (ii, 189). Each of these friends could expect affection mingled with a humorous dramatization of small events: 'Therefore I rarely write to you, tho' I often think of you. But another Reason is, that I doubt I know how to write *att* you: I might as well direct a Letter to the Sun, who when I rise, is at the East, & when I lie down, at the West. In my later Peregrinations, I heard of you every where, where you *Had been*; where you *was,* no mortal could tell....' (iv, 193). Again he tells Swift that the tireless septuagenarian, Sarah Duchess of Marlborough, 'makes great court to me, but I am too Old for her, Mind & body' (iv, 178). There is solicitude, fellow-feeling, delicate compliment, moving condolence.

But it is the early letters that really dazzle: above all, a superb report from Stanton Harcourt in Oxfordshire in the summer of 1718. Originally addressed to Lady Mary Wortley Montagu, it was reassigned on publication to the elderly man of affairs, Buckingham. This was both deceptive and misconceived, for the whole letter has a kind of *Rape of the Lock* quality – by turns gossipy, reflective, sensuous and fanciful. It is very much in Pope's 'feminine' manner, gradually building its effects from closely observed detail, and infused with a wistful melancholia he kept for the eyes of ladies. But it is also splendidly funny, and again it is not out of place to think of Dickens. Pope begins by describing the ramshackle layout of this 'genuine Ancient Country Seat', with a brewhouse where one would expect to find an imposing hall, and a sloping balcony 'which Time has turned to a very convenient Penthouse. The top is crown'd with a very venerable Tower, so like that of the Church just by, that the Jackdaws built in it as if it were the true Steeple'.

So the description proceeds, with a series of grotesque yet touching observations:

The great Hall is high & spatious, flankd with long tables (images of ancient hospitality) ornamented with monstrous horns, about 20 broken Pikes, & a match-lock Musquet or two, which they say were used in the Civil Wars. Here is one vast archd Window, beautifully darken'd with divers Scutcheons of painted Glass. There seems to be great propriety in this old manner of Blazoning upon Glass, Ancient Families being like ancient Windows, in the course of generations seldome free from Cracks. One shining Pane bears date 1286 : There the Face of Dame Elinor owes more to this single piece, than to all the Glasses she ever consulted in her life. Who can say after this, that Glass is frail, when it is not half so perishable as human Beauty, or Glory? For in another Pane you see the memory of a Knight preservd, whose marble Nose is molderd from his monument in the church adjoining. And yet, must not one sigh to reflect, that the most authentic record of so ancient a family shoud lye at the mercy of ev'ry Boy that throws a stone? In this Hall, in former days have dined Garterd Knights & Courtly Dames, with Ushers, Sewers, and Seneschalls; and yet it was but tother night that an Owl flew in hither, and mistook it for a Barn.

Then comes the parlour, lined with a historical tapestry, but now degraded to the function of storing dry poppies and mustard seed: 'The other contents of this room are a broken-belly'd Virginal, a couple of crippled Velvet chairs, with two or three mildewd pictures of mouldy Ancestors who look as dismally as if they came fresh from Hell with all their Brimstone about 'em.' In all there are twenty-four 'apartments' on the ground floor, including a pigeon house, a buttery, a dairy, a 'small Hole called the Chaplain's Study' and the 'Old Lady's Closet' with a lattice well-adapted for spying on servants.

On the upper floor the 'best room' is hung with cobwebs and the roof is so decayed that after a shower of rain a fine crop of mushrooms may be expected. Further, 'all this upper Story has for many years had no other Inhabitants than certain Rats, whose very Age renders them worthy of this venerable mansion, for the very Rats of this ancient Seat are gray. Since these have not yet quitted it, we hope at least this House may stand during the small remainder of days these poor animals have to live, who are now too infirm to move to another. They have still a small Subsistence left them, in the few remaining Books of the Library.' And then from this catalogue of decay, animate and inanimate, Pope moves neatly to his climax in the figure of an ancient retainer:

> I had never seen half what I have described, but for an old Starched grey headed Steward, who is much an Antiquity as any in the place, and looks like an old Family picture walked out of its Frame. He faild not as we past from room to room to relate several memoirs of the Family, but his obser- vations were particularly curious in the Cellar. He showd where stood the triple rows of Butts of Sack, & where were rang'd the bottles of Tent for Toasts in the morning. He pointed to the Stands that supported the Iron-hoop'd Hogs- heads of strong Beer. Then stepping to a corner, he lugg'd out the tattered fragment of an unframed Picture – This says he, with tears in his eyes, was poor Sir Thomas! once Master of all the Drink I told you of! He had two Sons, (poor young Masters) that never arrived to the Age of his Beer! They both fell ill in this very Cellar, and never went out upon their own legs.

The guide cannot pass by a broken bottle without showing the family arms engraved on it. Then up to the tower, by some dark winding steps:

> ...which landed us into several little Rooms. One of these was nailed up, and my Guide whisperd to me the occasion of it. It seems, the Course of this noble blood was interrupted about two Centuries ago, by a Freak of the Lady Frances, who was here taken up, & branded with the name of the Adultery-chamber. The Ghost of Lady Frances is supposed to walk here; some prying Maids of the family formerly reported that they saw a Lady in a fardingale thro' the key- hole; but this matter was hushd up. & the Servants forbid to speak of it. (i, 505–7)

At this point Pope breaks off, apologizing for his garrulity, and explaining that he has found it 'an excellent place for Re-

---

Tent   a red Spanish wine

tirement and Study', where he was able to get a great deal of Homer translated; 'Indeed I owe this old House the same sort of gratitude we do to an old friend, that harbours us in his declining condition, nay even in his last extremities.' – Pope squeezes every possible drop of meaning from the metaphor: it is relentlessly clever, but full of feeling too. Although he extracts fun from the old retainer, there are dignity and pathos present at the same time. In its assured rhythms and deftly mounted narrative, the letter can stand beside anything equivalent in our literature. It is a masterpiece of comic prose, enlisting to the full those attributes of the poet – in language as in description in comprehension as in wit – that Pope had laboured to acquire.

CHAPTER TEN

Pope and his age

It is no longer fashionable to speak of 'the age of Pope'. These days we prefer to stress tradition rather than individual talent: no single writer is willingly accorded preeminence within a complex period cut across by shifting currents of thought and feeling. We see Alexander Pope as an isolated hero, forging his own desperate sense of identity in a world threatening the stable order of civilization which he admired. And yet, as it often proves, the old orthodoxy had good sense in it. Pope *was* a representative writer of his time, to a far greater degree than Swift, Richardson or even Defoe. An outsider in the social sense, he was nonetheless able to infuse his best work with a sharp contemporary tang. Furthermore, he did not disdain the superficial polish of Augustan *vers de société*. Unlike Swift, he is rarely anguished; unlike Richardson, he seldom breaches the accepted canons of literary and emotional decorum; unlike Defoe, he maintains an eloquent and gentlemanly accent. He can be gross but he is never vulgar; he can be robust but he is never homely. In short, though his message is often subversive, his medium is generally conventional, dignified and untroubled. *The Rape of the Lock* is an object lesson in satiric technique; Belinda's world is comprehensively taken to pieces, yet the poem observes the polite code of that world with mocking exactitude.

Nor is it true that 'tradition' was purely a defence mechanism for Pope. He certainly disliked many features of his own time – the growing centralization of political and economic power, the development of the party system, the prestige accorded to textual scholarship, and much else. And sometimes he will appeal to a distant age for an image of heroic living. The key poem here is *The Dunciad,* with its buzz of epic allusion. But the crucial act on the part of Pope had derived from the years spent on Homer and Shakespeare, which had given him a wider sense of literary possibility than any other English writer of the eighteenth century. His predilection for Horace was a more personal thing, and indeed the imitations of Horace are the most direct and first-hand among all his works. And of course it was not only the ancient world that offered up 'classical' models for emulation, adaptation and allusion. As I have tried to show in earlier chapters, Chaucer, Spenser and Milton joined Shakespeare in a native pantheon; whilst Dryden provided Pope with constant challenge, stimulation and imaginative leadership. Pope was a great reader, and like many modern writers he read *creatively* – for his own purposes. It hurt him that Theobald could show him to be deficient as a technical scholar; but he drew from his editorial labours subjective and not objective skills. He was most truly himself as a poet when shadowed by the imaginary company of earlier masters.

In one particular respect Pope does appear to be an almost symbolic Augustan. This was in his passion for landscape gardening and devotion to the improvement of his small estate. Some have even thought his horticultural ideas 'romantic', and thus in some way at odds with his practice as a poet. But this view can hardly be sustained. The aesthetics of landscape gardening, with their emphasis on 'nature', taste, subordination of detail, and so on, were recognizably Augustan in origin and in feel. It is a historical accident that some of the expressive functions of a garden were similar to those later allotted to poetry, painting and music. Pope had announced his interest in the subject, along rather general lines, in a *Guardian* paper of 1713. However, it was not until he moved to Twickenham at the age of thirty that he devoted himself seriously to practical gardening. From the early 1720s onwards, it was nothing less than an obsession. The broad layout of his own garden was fixed within a few years, but that did not stop him tinkering and touching up for the rest of his days. Just as important, he became a kind of consultant to his friends. He may not have taken an active part in the design of Lord Cobham's intensely literary park at Stowe. But he certainly left critical comments on Lord Digby's at Sherborne, as we have seen (pp. 144–5 above), with a number of suggested improvements. He helped lay out the grounds at Marble Hill for his friend the Countess of Suffolk. He had some share in the development of Cirencester, owned by his close friend Bathurst; he assisted Ralph Allen at the sumptuous new Prior Park, near Bath; and he was also busy at Bevis Mount, near Southampton, and Wimpole in Cambridgeshire. His 'clients' were aristocrats, but they were also personal friends; and it should be remembered that along with the noble amateurs Pope had as his colleagues professional gardeners and designers – men like Charles Bridgman and William Kent.[1]

His response to architecture was less impassioned, though he certainly followed the impressive building activities of the Earl of Burlington with some interest. Nor did he apparently maintain his youthful addiction to painting (he actually took lessons from Charles Jervas for a year or so). He was always prepared to supervise some piece of monumental sculpture or to advise on the right placing of an epitaph. But in the visual arts as a whole his taste was pretty conventional. Only in his highly wrought garden, with its wealth of associative motifs, did he make any serious artistic statement to put alongside his poetry. The most important items here were the obelisk to the memory of his mother and the famous grotto. The latter summed up in its shell-lined tranquillity a whole attitude to literature and life. It was an allegorical picture of retirement, indeed of art itself: 'an undistinguishable Mixture of Realities and Imagery', grotto glooms and grotto glory – the still centre of Pope's dream of a happy existence.[2]

But Pope's need for retirement, as I have tried to show, was matched by an equally powerful urge to speak the truth about the world around him. It is sometimes implied that Pope was too moderate, too little of a party man, fully to share the ambitions of the Patriot Opposition in the 1730s. It seems to me, on the contrary, that he was perhaps more deeply imbued with its ideals than any other member of the group. His rejection of Walpole was not a matter of personal pique – indeed, the Prime Minister seems to have done Pope more than one good turn (quite apart from subscribing to the Homer!). It came rather from a pervasive depression over the state of the nation. Pope returns again and again to the baneful effects of moneyed men like Sir John Blunt, Dennis Bond, Peter Walter and John Ward. He believed that Walpole – the putative 'saviour' of the country after the calamitous Bubble – had in the event opened further avenues for the financial operator: the man who wheels and deals, rather than *making* anything. It is debatable as political history, but it does supply Pope with an angle, a consistent poetic vision. Years before, at the time of the Marlborough wars, Swift had argued that the new City institutions were shifting the moral centre of gravity in the nation. Pope expresses the same intuition, but not in generalized polemic or some hortatory prose essay. He takes instead particular persons and specific events, as in the boldly explicit *Epilogue to the Satires*. And even *The Dunciad,* with its mythic colouring and Grub Street locale, fixes historical processes with astonishing directness. Pope writes about the real world. That in itself is not a poetic virtue, but it is an essential condition for an imagination like Pope's to operate at white heat.

Nor, it is worth reminding ourselves, was Pope offering a petition for an absolute retreat. It was an essential factor in the dream that the poet should be settled in his chosen country, surrounded by a knot of special allies. Through the lapse of time the original Scriblerian formation had been destroyed. Nevertheless, Pope continued to value friendship as a cardinal element in the happy life; and he always required a sort of passive collaboration on the part of his acquaintances if his own work was to flourish (this is one reason for the highly revelatory nature of his correspondence). There can be nothing more misleading than to suppose that Pope was a perpetual loner, able to communicate with the men and women around him only through defiant gestures of art. He was in fact a highly *popular* poet from the start – and this came not just from personal notoriety (though he had that) but from a genuine rapport with his audience. He wrote about the things they were interested in, and he used a language that sounded pretty much like their own. *Windsor-Forest* is a public poem by reason of its patriotic theme, and also by reason of its clear, ringing, unesoteric delivery.

This is just where the difficulties begin for some modern readers. Conditioned by romantic training, they find it disturbing that a major writer should accommodate himself to the preferred forms of the day. It seems strange, in fact, that Pope can use the very accents of that society he exposed with so little mercy. And such readers are puzzled when the *Epistle to Arbuthnot,* at first sight an intensely personal (not to say autobio-

graphic) utterance, moves by degrees into something more
general and distanced. Again, the *Epistle to Augustus*, though
it draws on deeply felt first-hand experience, rests its case ultimately on a more 'public' set of historical facts, as in the discussion of poets as harmless 'madmen':

> Yet Sir, reflect, the mischief is not great;
> These Madmen never hurt the Church or State:
> Sometimes the Folly benefits mankind;
> And rarely Av'rice taints the tuneful mind.
> Allow him but his Play-thing of a Pen,
> He ne'er rebels, or plots, like other men:
> Flight of Cashiers, or Mobs, he'll never mind;
> And knows no losses while the Muse is kind.
> To cheat a Friend, or Ward, he leaves to Peter;
> The good man heaps up nothing but mere metre,
> Enjoys his Garden and his Book in quiet;
> And then – a perfect Hermit in his Diet.
> Of little use the Man you may suppose,
> Who says in verse what others say in prose;
> Yet let me show, a Poet's of some weight,
> And (tho' no Soldier) useful to the State.
> What will a Child learn sooner than a song?
> What better teach a Foreigner the tongue?
> What's long or short, each accent where to place,
> And speak in publick with some sort of grace.
> I scarce can think him such a worthless thing,
> Unless he praise some monster of a King.
> Or Virtue, or Religion turn to sport,
> To please a lewd, or un-believing Court.
>
> (189–212)

Here Pope ironically accepts the popular image of a neutered
court poet, producing innocent entertainment with his childish
'plaything of a pen'. Finally, there is the long-drawn battle
between those 'mighty opposites', Pope and Robert Walpole,
where again the private skirmishes act out a larger political
and cultural battle.[3]

Ward, Peter   corrupt and crooked financiers

A related point here. We expect the artist's vision to be skewed and idiosyncratic, not just for added piquancy, but because (we like to think) this is the way to uncover the deepest truths. So Lord Clark tells us that impressionist landscapes really show us the way things are, instead of the 'false' verisimilitude of Victorian naturalist painting.[4] Men and women in Pope's day would not have easily been convinced. They mostly thought that the everyday perceptions of reasonably educated people offered reliable versions of reality. They could construe the most influential philosopher of the age, John Locke, to say as much. Bishop Berkeley, who was supposed to have said the opposite, they did not pretend to understand. And so they wanted their artists to express in memorable form these same perceptions. They did not want poetry to be a hieratic activity, full of codes and ciphers, as the Elizabethans had desired it. They did not see it as intellectual play, as had the Metaphysicals. Instead, they wanted a literature for the average, not too sensual man; and they were suspicious of unduly elevated claims for the mysterious or transcendental in art.

Of course, Pope – being a great writer – did not deliver exactly what his audience had ordered. There *are* codes and secret messages in his work; there is a constant thread of myth, irrationality and fancy – as earlier chapters should have indicated. But he was sufficiently a man of his time not to be cramped by these prevalent expectations. He found intractable neither the subject-matter nor the poetic idiom then in fashion:

> She went, to plain-work, and to purling brooks,
> Old-fashion'd halls, dull aunts, and croaking rooks,
> She went from Op'ra, park, assembly, play,
> To morning walks, and pray'rs three hours a day;
> To pass her time 'twixt reading and Bohea,
> To muse, and spill her solitary Tea,
> Or o'er cold coffee trifle with the spoon,
> Count the slow clock, and dine exact at noon;
> Divert her eyes with pictures in the fire,
> Hum half a tune, tell stories to the squire;

Bohea   a sort of tea

> Up to her godly garret after sev'n,
> There starve and pray, for that's the way to heav'n...
> In some fair evening, on your elbow laid,
> You dream of triumphs in the rural shade;
> In pensive thought recall the fancy'd scene,
> See Coronations rise on ev'ry green;
> Before you pass th' imaginary sights
> Of Lords, and Earls, and Dukes, and garter'd Knights;
> While the spread Fan o'ershades your closing eyes;
> Then gave one flirt, and all the vision flies.
> Thus vanish sceptres, coronets, and balls,
> And leave you in lone woods, or empty walls.
>
> (*Epistle to Miss Blount*, 11–22, 31–40)

In this poem Pope is describing the boredom of a young girl banished to the country after an exciting trip to town for the coronation of George I. The technique is masterly: it could only proceed from a writer deeply at home with his inherited medium. Note how closely we are placed to the physical details: the langorous pose on one elbow, the eyes 'closing' but, the impulse half-resisted, not quite shut. Pope makes the very rhythm enact the weariness felt by this mooning girl – the line 'Up to her godly garret after sev'n' suggests an automatic plod up an endless staircase to the uninviting (and all too empty) bedroom. 'After sev'n' has somehow become very late – it has taken so long for the clock (like this line) to reach it. Yet again we see Pope starting from the scraps of society chitchat – earls and dukes, coffee spoons, operas and balls – and then passing to a more inward realm of make believe and self-communion.

It is paradoxical that no one is better than Pope, the textbook example of a 'social' poet, at rendering these dramas of our everyday existence. He *knows* about people – even, one half-reluctantly concedes, knows about you and me. Sometimes, perhaps, the pleasures of Pope are slightly guilty ones, when one finds a too-ready complicity in destroying with him the infamous of this world. But read on a few pages, and one finds that the target is shifted. It is no longer the remote eighteenth-century speculator who is under fire: now it is the would-be Lothario, or the pettish girl, or the belated adolescent. Sooner or later, the cap fits. Aesthetically, Pope is a joy for ever; but he is too observant and knowledgeable always to make comfortable reading. Like the society he wrote about, and for, we can never take it for granted he is on our side.

ABBREVIATIONS

The following short forms are used in the text and in the notes at the end:

Corr	*The Correspondence of Alexander Pope*, ed. G. Sherburn (Oxford, 1956).
MS	*The Memoirs of Martinus Scriblerus*, ed. C. Kerby-Miller (New Haven, 1950).
PB	*Peri Bathous*, ed. E. L. Steeves (New York, 1952).
Prose	*The Prose Works of Alexander Pope,* ed. N. Ault (Oxford, 1936).
Sherburn	G. Sherburn, *The Early Career of Alexander Pope* (Oxford, 1934).
TE	The Twickenham Edition of *The Poems of Alexander Pope,* gen. ed. J. Butt (London, 1939–69). This is the text used throughout. Individual works are abbreviated as follows:

	Dun	*The Dunciad*
	EA	*Epistle to Dr Artbuthnot*
	EOC	*Essay on Criticism*
	EOM	*Essay on Man*
	IH	*Imitations of Horace*
	Il	*The Iliad* (in Pope's translation)
	ME	*Moral Essays*
	Od	*The Odyssey* (in Pope's translation)
	Past	*Pastorals*
	ROL	*Rape of the Lock*
	TF	*Temple of Fame*
	WF	*Windsor-Forest*

The following abbreviations are used in the notes alone:

CH	*Pope: The Critical Heritage,* ed. J. Barnard (London and Boston, 1973).
DIXON	*Writers and their Background: Alexander Pope*, ed. P. Dixon (London, 1972).
EssA	*Essential Articles for the Study of Alexander Pope,* ed. M. Mack (Hamden, Conn., 2nd edn 1968).
GS	P. Rogers, *Grub Street: Studies in a Subculture* (London, 1972).
SPENCE	Joseph Spence, *Observations, Anecdotes, and Characters of Books and Men,* ed. J. M. Osborn (Oxford, 1966).
WILLIAMS	A. Williams, *Pope's Dunciad* (London, 1955).
EIC	*Essays in Criticism*

ECS	*Eighteenth Century Studies*
HLQ	*Huntington Library Quarterly*
JEGP	*Journal of English and Germanic Philology*
MLQ	*Modern Language Quarterly*
MP	*Modern Philology*
PBA	*Proceedings of the British Academy*
PQ	*Philological Quarterly*
PMLA	*PMLA: Publications of the Modern Language Association of America*
RES	*Review of English Literature 1500–1900*
SEL	*Studies in English Literature 1500–1900*
TLS	*Times Literary Supplement*
TSLL	*Texas Studies in Literature and Language*

NOTES

CHAPTER 1

1 I have developed this view in an essay on 'Pope and the Social Scene', DIXON, pp. 101–5.
2 See M. H. Nicolson and G. S. Rousseau, *This Long Disease, My Life* (Princeton, 1968), for the best account of Pope's health.
3 DIXON, p. 142.
4 See Agnes M. Sibley, *Alexander Pope's Prestige in America, 1725–1835* (New York, 1949).
5 M. Mack, 'Alexander Pope', in *Pope: Twentieth Century Views,* ed. J. V. Guerinot (Englewood Cliffs, N.J., 1972), p. 49.

CHAPTER 2

1 See my article 'Pope and the Syntax of Satire', *Literary English Since Shakespeare,* ed. G. Watson (New York, 1970), pp. 236–65; and, more generally, J. A. Jones, *Pope's Couplet Art* (Athens, Ohio, 1969).
2 W. K. Wimsatt, *The Verbal Icon* (London, 1970), p. 180.
3 See I. Ehrenpreis, 'The Style of Sound: the Literary Value of Pope's Versification', *The Augustan Milieu,* ed. H. K. Miller, E. Rothstein and G. S. Rousseau (Oxford, 1970), pp. 232–46, esp. pp. 244–5.
4 G. Tillotson, *On the Poetry of Pope* (Oxford, 2nd edn 1950), p. 116.

CHAPTER 3

1 *CH,* p. 384.
2 *EssA,* p. 151.
3 R. A. Brower, *Alexander Pope: The Poetry of Allusion* (Oxford, 1959), p. 39. Brower's remains the best general introduction to the poems.
4 *Lives of the English Poets,* ed. G. B. Hill (Oxford, 1905), I, 77.
5 See my article, 'A Pope Family Scandal', *TLS,* 31 August 1973, p. 1005; the reply by E. P. Thompson, 'Alexander Pope and the Berkshire Blacks', *TLS,* 7 September 1973, pp. 1031–3; and subsequent correspondence in *TLS.*
6 *EssA,* pp. 209–10. Empson amends his argument to some extent in his *Structure of Complex Words* (London, 1951), pp. 99–100, but still, in my view, understates the importance of *sense* in the poem.

CHAPTER 4

1 See my article, 'Faery Lore in *The Rape of the Lock,'RES,* XXV (1974), 25–38.

2 T. R. Edwards, *This Dark Estate* (Berkeley, 1963), p. 21. For another view of Pope's attitudes to the world of Belinda, see my article, 'Wit and Grammar in *The Rape of the Lock*', *JEGP*, LXXII (1973), 17–31.

3 G. Wilson Knight, *The Poetry of Alexander Pope, Laureate of Peace* (London, 1965), pp. 79–110. The book first appeared in 1955.

4 Brower, op. cit., p. 94.

5 TE, II, 225.

6 J. P. Russo, *Alexander Pope: Tradition and Identity* (Cambridge, Mass., 1972), p. 139, calls the preface 'unremitting' and 'fairly humorless', an opinion which others share.

CHAPTER 5

1 See TE, VII, cvii–clxiii. The best survey of the Homer enterprise is found in the Introduction by M. Mack *et al.* to TE, VII. See also R. A. Brower, *Alexander Pope: The Poetry of Allusion* (Oxford, 1959), pp. 85–135. Pope's own comments are found in SPENCE, I, 82–90.

2 TE, VII, lxiii. See also VII, cciv–ccv, on Pope's determination to preserve his own idiom, and on the differences from Homeric style this entailed. A comparable argument is advanced by Leslie Stephen – that Pope's voice was 'more or less a falsetto', but authentic in its way. See Stephen's *Alexander Pope* (London, 1888), pp. 70–1.

3 J. Arthos, *The Language of Natural Description in Eighteenth-Century Poetry* (Ann Arbor, 1949), pp. 25–6.

4 TE, VII, lxv–lxvii.

5 The text followed is that of *Eighteenth Century Essays on Shakespeare*, ed. D. Nichol Smith, (Oxford, 2nd edn 1963), pp. 44–58.

6 For this exchange, see T. R. Lounsbury, *The Text of Shakespeare* (London, 1906).

7 See S. Schoenbaum, *Shakespeare's Lives* (Oxford, 1970), pp. 149–53.

8 See J. Butt, *Pope's Taste in Shakespeare* (London, 1935); P. Dixon, 'Pope's Shakespeare', *JEGP*, LXIII (1964), 191–203; and J. M. Newton, 'Alive or Dead?', *Cambridge Quarterly*, III (1968), 267–73. Among passages particularly admired by Pope were the Duke's speech at the start of Act II in *As You Like It*, the scene in *The Tempest* in which Caliban meets Trinculo and Stephano, and Isabella's rebuke to Angelo – as well as a number of high points in the tragedies. Surprisingly, Pope thought *Love's Labour's Lost* 'the worst of his plays' (*Corr.*, iv, 475).

9 Loundsbury, *Text*, pp. 86–93, offers a much harsher estimate than mine of the value of Pope's explanatory glosses.

10 DIXON, p. 34. For the relevance of the Homer to Pope's 'original' poetry, see TE, VII, ccxi–ccxlix.

CHAPTER 6

1 For this phase see *CH,* pp. 217–86.

2 See G. Sherburn, 'Pope and "The Great Shew of Nature" ', *The Seventeenth Century,* ed. R. F. Jones (Stanford, 1951), pp. 314–15; and, for the background, A. O. Lovejoy, *The Great Chain of Being* (Baltimore, 1936), pp. 183–207.

3 P. Dixon, *The World of Pope's Satires* (London, 1968), pp. 41–52, provides a most helpful commentary on this point.

4 For this aspect of Augustan taste, see M. Mack, *The Garden and the City* (Toronto, 1969), pp. 21–5; and J. D. Hunt, 'Emblem and expressionism in the eighteenth-century landscape garden', *ECS,* IV (1971), 294–317.

5 TE, III, ii, xxxiv: but see SPENCE, I, 129, where the remark is applied to the first epistle of the *Essay on Man.*

6 See H. Erskine-Hill, 'Pope and the Financial Revolution', DIXON, pp. 200–29.

7 TE, III, ii, 164–8. For a more recent view, identifying Timon with Robert Walpole, see K. Mahaffey, 'Timon's Villa', *TSLL,* IX (1967), 193–222.

CHAPTER 7

1 Of the vast library of works on Horace, perhaps the most directly useful to a student of Pope are: N. Rudd, *The Satires of Horace* (Cambridge, 1966); C. D. N. Costa (ed.), *Horace* (London, 1973) (see esp. O. A. W. Dilke, 'Horace and the Verse Letter', pp. 94–112); and C. O. Brink, *Horace on Poetry* (Cambridge, 1963). Standard, though a little technical, is E. Frankel, *Horace* (Oxford, 1957); whilst an older book by A. Y. Campbell, *Horace: A New Interpretation* (London, 1924), remains provocative. For the concept of 'imitation', see a good study by H. Weinbrot, *The Formal Strain* (Chicago, 1969).

2 J. V. Guerinot (ed.), *Pope: Twentieth Century Views* (Englewood Cliffs, N.J., 1972), p. 49.

3 Camille A. Paglia, 'Lord Hervey and Pope', *ECS,* VI (1973), 348–71.

4 See my article, 'A Drama of Mixed Feelings', *The Use of English,* XXV (1973), 142–6.

5 J. M. Osborn, 'Pope, the Byzantine Empress, and Walpole's Whore', *EssA,* pp. 580–8.

6 R. A. Brower, *Alexander Pope: The Poetry of Allusion* (Oxford, 1959), p. 313.

7 I. Jack, 'Pope and ... Donne's Satires', *EssA,* p. 426.

CHAPTER 8

1 M. McLuhan, *The Gutenberg Galaxy* (1962), cited in F. W. Bateson

and N. A. Joukovsky (eds.), *Pope: A Critical Anthology* (Harmonds-worth, 1971), p. 440.

2 TE, V, xliii–xlviii. Unless otherwise stated, references in this chapter are to the 'B' text of 1743.

3 TE, V, xlii.

4 WILLIAMS, pp. 17–25.

5 WILLIAMS, pp. 42–8.

6 WILLIAMS, pp. 141, 143.

7 WILLIAMS, pp. 30–41; see also *GS*, pp. 70–6.

8 *GS*, p. 166; for riots, see *GS*, pp. 99–126.

9 This case is developed in *GS*, pp. 56–62.

10 WILLIAMS, pp. 87–103; see also my article, 'The Critique of Opera in Pope's *Dunciad*', *Musical Quarterly*, LIX (1973), 15–30.

11 J. V. Guerinot (ed.), *Pope: Twentieth Century Views* (Englewood Cliffs, N.J., 1972), pp. 125–6.

12 See M. Rosenblum, 'Pope's Illusive Temple of Infamy', *The Satirist's Art*, ed. J. H. Jensen and M. R. Zirker (Bloomington, 1972), pp. 28–54.

13 I. Jack, *Augustan Satire* (Oxford, 1952), p. 134.

14 *EssA*, pp. 803–24.

15 *CH*, p. 517.

16 *EssA*, pp. 730–46.

17 J. E. Sitter, *The Poetry of Pope's Dunciad* (Minneapolis, 1971), p. 9.

18 Sitter, op. cit., p. 84.

19 TE, V, xxxii–xxxvii; see also Jack, *Satire*, pp. 123–4.

20 J. A. Jones, *Pope's Couplet Art* (Athens, Ohio, 1969), p. 147.

21 Guerinot, op. cit., pp. 127, 147.

22 *EssA*, pp. 808–15; see the same author's *Pope: The Dunciad* (London, 1972), pp. 27–37, for a restatement of this case.

23 Sitter, op. cit., pp. 10–50, discusses miscegenation; for the lines on Norton see *GS*, p. 313.

24 For this motif see A. D. Nuttall, 'Fishes in the Trees', *EIC*, XXIV (1974), 20–38.

25 *EssA*, p. 810.

CHAPTER 9

1 See *Prose*, xxxviii–lv; and D. F. Bond (ed.), *The Spectator* (Oxford, 1965), I, xlviii–xlix.

2 For the best account see *MS*, 1–56.

3 Quoted in *MS*, 43.

4 For the relevance of this 'sublime' to Pope's own Homer, see *PB*, lviii–lxiii.

5 *Corr*, i, xiii. The narrative of these events by Sherburn (i, xi–xviii) as illuminating though perhaps too brief.

6 See Mack's review of *Corr* in *PQ*, XXXVI (1967), 394–6.

7 Rosemary Cowler, 'Shadow and Substance: A Discussion of Pope's Correspondence', *The Familiar Letter in the Eighteenth Century*, ed. H. Anderson *et al.* (Lawrence, Kansas, 1966), p. 45. I am in much closer accord with Professor Cowler's remark that the letters 'almost all have one thing in common – the projection of a man' (p. 37).

CHAPTER 10

1 For a good discussion, see James Sambrook, 'Pope and the Visual Arts', DIXON, pp. 143–71.

2 See M. Mack, *The Garden and the City* (Toronto, 1969), pp. 41–76.

3 See Mack, op. cit., pp. 188–231.

4 Kenneth Clark, *Landscape into Art* (Harmondsworth, 1956), pp. 100–101.

READING LIST

(* indicates that an edition in paperback is available)

REFERENCE

R. H. GRIFFITH, *Alexander Pope: A Bibliography*, 2 vols (Austin, Texas, 1922–7).

J. V. GUERINOT, *Pamphlet Attacks on Alexander Pope, 1711–1744: A Descriptive Bibliography* (London, 1969).

V. A. DEARING, 'Alexander Pope', *New Cambridge Bibliography of English Literature,* ed. G. Watson, II (Cambridge, 1971), 500–27.

EDITIONS

J. BUTT *et al.* (ed.), *The Twickenham Edition of the Poems of Alexander Pope*, 11 vols (London and New Haven, 1939–69). (* A one-volume text, ed. Butt (1963).)

W. ELWIN and W. J. COURTHOPE (eds.), *The Works of Alexander Pope*, 10 vols (London, 1871–89).

H. DAVIS (ed.), *The Poetical Works of Alexander Pope* (Oxford, 1966).

G. SHERBURN (ed.), *The Correspondence of Alexander Pope*, 5 vols (Oxford, 1956).

N. AULT (ed.), *The Prose Works of Alexander Pope* (Oxford, 1936). Only 1 vol. published.

C. KERBY-MILLER (ed.), *Memoirs of the Life of Martinus Scriblerus* (New Haven, 1950).

E. L. STEEVES (ed.), *The Art of Sinking in Poetry* (New York, 1952).

*B. A. GOLDGAR (ed.), *The Literary Criticism of Alexander Pope* (Lincoln, Nebraska, 1965).

R. MORTON and W. M. PETERSON (eds.), *Three Hours after Marriage* (Painesville, Ohio, 1965).

BIOGRAPHY

G. SHERBURN, *The Early Career of Alexander Pope* (Oxford, 1934).

N. AULT, *New Light on Pope* (London, 1949).

*B. DOBRÉE, *Alexander Pope* (London, 1951).

P. QUENNELL, *Alexander Pope: The Education of a Genius 1688–1728* (London, 1968).

M. H. NICOLSON and G. S. ROUSSEAU, *This Long Disease, My Life* (Princeton, 1968).

JOSEPH SPENCE, *Observations, Anecdotes, and Characters of Books and Men,* ed. J. M. Osborn, 2 vols (Oxford, 1966).

AIDS TO STUDY

E. ABBOTT, *A Concordance to the Works of Pope* (London, 1875).

J. BARNARD (ed.), *Pope: The Critical Heritage* (London and Boston, 1973).

*F. W. BATESON and N. A. JOUKOVSKY (eds.), *Pope: A Critical Anthology* (Harmondsworth, 1971).

M. MACK (ed.), *Essential Articles for the Study of Alexander Pope* (Hamden, Conn., 2nd edn 1968).

P. DIXON (ed.), *Writers and their Background: Alexander Pope* (London, 1972).

W. K. WIMSATT, *The Portraits of Alexander Pope* (New Haven, 1965).

GENERAL CRITICISM (books only)

B. BOYCE, *The Character-Sketches in Pope's Poems* (Durham, N.C., 1962).

*R. A. BROWER, *Alexander Pope: the Poetry of Allusion* (Oxford, 1959).

T. R. EDWARDS, *This Dark Estate: A Reading of Pope* (Berkeley, 1963).

*E. GURR, *Pope* (Edinburgh, 1971).

*G. WILSON KNIGHT, *The Poetry of Pope, Laureate of Peace* (London, 1965).

M. MACK, *The Garden and the City: Retirement and Politics in the Later Poetry of Pope, 1731–1743* (Toronto, 1969).

R. W. ROGERS, *The Major Satires of Alexander Pope* (Urbana, Ill., 1955).

J. P. RUSSO, *Alexander Pope: Tradition and Identity* (Cambridge, Mass., 1972).

G. TILLOTSON, *Pope and Human Nature* (Oxford, 1958).

A. WARREN, *Alexander Pope as Critic and Humanist* (Princeton, 1929).

BACKGROUND

J. CHALKER, *The English Georgic* (London, 1969).

*P. FUSSELL, *The Rhetorical World of Augustan Humanism* (Oxford, 1965).

*I. JACK, *Augustan Satire* (Oxford, 1952).

A. B. KERNAN, *The Plot of Satire* (New Haven, 1965).

*M. PRICE, *To the Palace of Wisdom* (New York, 1964).

P. ROGERS, *Grub Street: Studies in a Subculture* (London, 1972).

R. TRICKETT, *The Honest Muse: A study in Augustan Verse* (Oxford, 1967).

H. D. WEINBROT, *The Formal Strain: Studies in Augustan Imitation and Satire* (Chicago, 1969).

PARTICULAR STUDIES

1   The writer and his audience

A. BELJAME, *Men of Letters and the English Public 1660–1744*, tr. E. O. Lorimer (London, 1948).

* A. R. HUMPHREYS, *The Augustan World* (London, 1955).

*I. WATT (ed.), *The Augustan Age* (Greenwich, Conn., 1968).

P. ROGERS, *The Augustan Vision* (London, 1974).

2   The politics of style

J. A. JONES, *Pope's Couplet Art* (Athens, Ohio, 1969).

R. P. PARKIN, *The Poetic Workmanship of Alexander Pope* (Minneapolis, 1955).

J. H. ADLER, *The Reach of Art: A Study in the Prosody of Pope* (Gainesville, Fla., 1964).

P. M. SPACKS, *An Argument of Images: the Poetry of Alexander Pope* (Cambridge, Mass., 1971).

G. TILLOTSON, *On the Poetry of Pope* (Oxford, 2nd edn, 1950).

E. OLSON, 'Rhetoric and Appreciation of Pope', *MP*, XXXVII (1939), 13–35.

P. ROGERS, 'Pope and the Syntax of Satire', *Literary English since Shakespeare*, ed. G. Watson (New York, 1970), pp. 236–65.

*W. K. WIMSATT, 'One Relation of Rhyme to Reason: Alexander Pope' and 'Rhetoric and Poems: Alexander Pope' in *The Verbal Icon* (London, 1970), pp. 153–85

3   Soft numbers and good sense

G. MELCHIORI, 'Pope in Arcady', *English Miscellany*, XIV (1963), 83–93 *(EssA)*

W. EMPSON, 'Wit in the *Essay on Criticism*', in *The Structure of Complex Words* (London, 1951), pp. 84–100 *(EssA)*.

*E. N. HOOKER, 'Pope on Wit: the *Essay on Criticism*', in *The Seventeenth Century*, ed. R. F. Jones (Stanford, 1951), pp. 225–46 *(EssA)*.

P. RAMSEY, 'The Watch of Judgement: Relativism and *An Essay on Criticism*', in *Studies in Criticism and Aesthetics 1660–1800*, ed. H. Anderson and J. S. Shea (Minneapolis, 1967), pp. 128–39.

*E. R. WASSERMANN, '*Windsor Forest*', in *The Subtler Language* (Baltimore, 1959) pp. 101–68.

P. ROGERS, 'The Enamelled Ground: the Language of Heraldry and Natural Description in *Windsor-Forest*', *Studia Neophilologica*, XLV (1973), 356–71.

R. M. SCHMITZ, *Pope's Windsor-Forest 1712* (St Louis, 1952).

4   Fancy's maze

*J. S. CUNNINGHAM, *Pope: The Rape of the Lock* (London, 1961).

*G. S. ROUSSEAU (ed.), *Twentieth Century Interpretations of The Rape of the Lock* (Englewood Cliffs, N.J., 1969).

*J. D. HUNT, (ed.), *The Rape of the Lock: A Casebook* (London, 1968).

A. L. WILLIAMS, 'The Fall of China and *The Rape of the Lock*', *PQ,* LXI (1962), 412–25 *(EssA)*.

E. R. WASSERMANN, 'The Limits of Allusion in *The Rape of the Lock*', *JEGP,* LXV (1966), 425–44.

P. ROGERS, 'Faery Lore in *The Rape of the Lock*', *RES*, XXV (1974), 25–38.

M. KRIEGER, 'Eloisa to Abelard : the Escape from Body or the Embrace of Body', *ECS*, III (1969), 28–47.

5 Homer and Shakespeare

R. SÜHNEL, *Homer und die englische Humanität* (Tübingen, 1958).

D. KNIGHT, *Pope and the Heroic Tradition* (New Haven, 1951).

W. FROST, '*The Rape of the Lock* and Pope's Homer', *MLQ*, VIII (1947), 342–52 (*EssA*).

J. BUTT, *Pope's Taste in Shakespeare* (London, 1935).

P. DIXON, 'Pope's Shakespeare', *JEGP*, LXIII (1964), 191–203.

J. M. NEWTON, 'Alive or Dead ?' *Cambridge Quarterly*, III, (1968). 267–273.

J. SUTHERLAND, 'The Dull Duty of an Editor', *RES*, XXI (1945), 202–215 (*EssA*).

6 Maps of humanity

M. KALLICH, *Heav'n's First Law* (De Kalb, Illinois, 1967).

D. H. WHITE, *Pope and the Context of Controversy* (Chicago, 1970).

M. MACK (ed.), *An Essay on Man* (Oxford, 1962).

F. E. L. PRIESTLEY, 'Pope and the Great Chain of Being', *Essays in English Literature from the Renaissance to the Victorian Age*, ed. M. MacLure and F. W. Watt (Toronto, 1964), pp. 213–28.

F. BRADY, 'The History and Structure of Pope's *To a Lady*', *SEL*, IX (1969), 439–62.

E. R. WASSERMANN, *Pope's 'Epistle to Bathurst': A Critical Reading* (Baltimore, 1960).

7 Images of Life

T. MARESCA, *Pope's Horatian Poems* (Columbus, Ohio, 1966).

J. M. ADEN, *Something like Horace* (Nashville, 1969).

*P. DIXON, *The World of Pope's Satires* (London, 1968).

J. M. OSBORN, 'Pope, the Byzantine Empress, and Walpole's Whore', *RES*, VI (1955), 372–82 (*EssA*).

I. JACK, 'Pope and "the Weighty Bullion of Dr Donne's Satires" ', *PMLA*, LXVI (1951), 1009–22 (*EssA*).

H. ERSKINE-HILL, 'Courtiers out of Horace', *John Donne : Essays in Celebration*, ed. A. J. Smith (London, 1972), pp. 273–307.

M. SCHONHORN, 'The Audacious Contemporaneity of Pope's *Epistle to Augustus*', *SEL*, VII (1968), 431–43.

8 The empire of dulness

A. L. WILLIAMS, *Pope's 'Dunciad': A Study of its Meaning* (London, 1955).

J. E. SITTER, *The Poetry of Pope's 'Dunciad'* (Minneapolis, 1971).

*H. ERSKINE-HILL, *Pope: The Dunciad* (London, 1972).

M. ROSENBLUM, 'Pope's Illusive Temple of Infamy', *The Satirist's Art,* ed. J. H. Jenson and M. R. Zirker (Bloomington, 1972), pp. 28–54.

E. JONES, 'Pope and Dulness', *PBA,* LIV (1969), 232–63.

P. ROGERS, 'The Name and Nature of Dulness,' *Anglia,* XCII (1974), 79–112.

W. KINSLEY, 'The *Dvnciad* as Mock-Book', *HLQ,* XXXV (1971), 29–47.

E. F. MENGEL JR, 'The *Dunciad* Illustrations', *ECS,* VII (1973). 161–78.

G. SHERBURN, 'The *Dunciad,* Book IV', *TSLL,* XXIV (1944), 174–90 (*EssA*).

9 A poet's prose

M. GOLDSTEIN, *Pope and the Augustan Stage* (Stanford, 1958).

G. SHERBURN, 'The Fortunes and Misfortunes of *Three Hours after Marriage*', *MP,* XXIV (1926), 91–109.

*R. COWLER, 'Shadow and Substance: A Discussion of Pope's Correspondence', *The Familiar Letter in the Eighteenth Century*, ed. H. Anderson, P. B. Daghlian, I. Ehrenpreis (Lawrence, Kansas, 1966), pp. 34–48.

J. BUTT, 'Pope Seen Through his Letters', *Eighteenth-Century English Literature: Modern Essays in Criticism* (New York, 1959), pp. 62–7.

10 Pope and his age

M. MACK, 'On Reading Pope', *College English,* VII (1946), 263–73.

M. MACK, 'Wit and Poetry and Pope', *Pope and his Contemporaries,* ed. J. L. Clifford and L. A. Landa (Oxford, 1949), pp. 20–40.

M. MACK, 'The Muse of Satire', *Yale Review,* XLI (1951), 80–92.

G. SHERBURN, 'Pope and "The Great Shew of Nature" ', in *The Seventeenth Century,* ed. R. F. Jones (Stanford, 1951), pp. 306–15.

W. H. AUDEN, 'Alexander Pope', *From Anne to Victoria,* ed. B. Dobrée (London, 1937), pp. 89–107 (*EssA*).

TABLE OF DATES

	POPE'S AGE	WORKS	OTHER EVENTS
1688	P. born in London 21 May.		Protestant Revolution.
c. 1698–1701	10–13		P.'s family move from London to Binfield (in Windsor Forest).
1702	14		Queen Anne comes to throne.
1704	16		Battle of Blenheim; Swift: *A Tale of a Tub*.
1707	19		Union with Scotland.
1709	21	*Pastorals*	
1710	22		Sacheverell affair, leading to formation of Harley's Tory government.
1711	23	*Essay on Criticism*	The *Spectator* begins publication (P. occasional contributor).
1712	24	*The Rape of the Lock* (first version in two cantos); *The Messiah*	Handel settles in London.
1713	25	*Windsor-Forest*	Peace of Utrecht.
1714	26	*The Rape of the Lock* (in five cantos)	Hanovarian accession; Tories lose power.
1715	27	*Iliad* vol. I; *The Temple of Fame*	Jacobite rising of 'Old Pretender'.
1716	28	*Iliad*, vol. II	P.'s family move to Chiswick.
1717	29	*Works; Iliad* vol. III	P.'s father dies.
1718	30	*Iliad* vol. IV	Parnell dies; P. moves to Twickenham.
1719	31		Defoe: *Robinson Crusoe*.
1720	32	*Iliad* vols. V & VI	South Sea Bubble.
1721	33	Edition of Parnell	Walpole comes to power.
1722	34		Defoe: *Moll Flanders*; Atterbury affair breaks out.

1723	35	Edition of Buckingham	Atterbury exiled; P.'s brother-in-law arrested for deer-stealing.
1724	36		Swift: *Drapier's Letters*.
1725	37	*Odyssey* vols. I–III; Edition of Shakespeare	
1726	38	*Odyssey* vols. IV–V	Swift visits England and publishes *Gulliver's Travels*.
1727	39	Pope–Swift *Miscellanies* vols. I–II	Accession of George II.
1728	40	*The Dunciad* (first version); *Peri Bathous*	Gay: *The Beggar's Opera*.
1729	41	*The Dunciad Variorum*	
1730	42		Thomson: *The Seasons*; Fielding: *The Author's Farce*.
1731	43	*Epistle to Burlington*	Defoe dies.
1732	44	Pope–Swift *Miscellanies* vol. 'III'	Gay dies; Atterbury dies; Hogarth: *The Harlot's Progress*.
1733	45	*Epistle to Bathurst*; first of *Imitations of Horace*; *Essay on Man* I–III	P.'s mother dies.
1734	46	*Essay on Man* IV; *Epistle to Cobham*	
1735	47	*Epistle to Arbuthnot*; *Epistle to a Lady*; Curll's edition of *Letters*	Arbuthnot dies; Hogarth: *Rake's Progress*.
1736	48		Fielding's play *Pasquin*.
1737	49	*Letters* (authorised edition); *Epistle to Augustus*	Theatrical Licensing Act; Queen Caroline dies.
1738	50	*Epilogue to the Satires*	Samuel Johnson: *London* (admired by P.).
1739	51		Hume: *Treatise of Human Nature* (Books I–II).
1740	52		Richardson: *Pamela*; Cibber's *Apology*.

1741	53	*Memoirs of Scriblerus*	Fielding: *Shamela*
1742	54	*The Dunciad* Book IV (separately)	Fielding: *Joseph Andrews*; Handel: *The Messiah*; fall of Walpole.
1743	55	*The Dunciad in Four Books*	
1744	56 P. dies, 30 May		Johnson: *Life of Savage*.
1745	—		Swift dies; Walpole dies; Hogarth: *Marriage à la Mode*; Jacobite rising of young Pretender.

Index